SUCCESS through MANIPULATION

Subconscious Reactions That Will Make or Break You

Colin Christopher

MANCHESTER HOUSE
PUBLISHING

SUCCESS through MANIPULATION
Subconscious Reactions That Will Make or Break You

Colin Christopher

Published by
Manchester House Publishing
www.manchesterhousepublishing.com

ISBN: 978-0-9917612-0-3

Credits
Editor: Brenda Robinson
www.potentpen.com

Jacket and Book design by Chris Simon
Hotspot Creative Solutions
www.hotspotcreative.ca

Dedication

This book is dedicated to my family.

To my mother, Herta Weiss. Your support through all the years for my upbringing, wellbeing and education will always be remembered. I realize it wasn't easy for you and I appreciate everything you've done and the sacrifices you've made. I love you.

To my father, Emil Weiss. Thank you for the little things that you always do to help me out. I know they're not glamorous, and I wish I would say thank you more, but I value your help. I love you.

To my brother Norbert Weiss. What can I say to the guy that I grew up wanting to be like? Being ten years older than me, I know you had other things going on with your friends and hanging out with your little brother wasn't on the top of your list. But it's always great to see and talk to you. It always meant a lot when you included me, and it always will. I love you.

Acknowledgements

To all the people I've hypnotized, from hypnosis shows to the hypnotherapy chair and everyone in between, you inspire me!

To Anny Slegten, my hypnosis teacher, you've taught me so much and your wisdom has enabled me to help others.

To Sheldon Fingler, my colleague and friend, brainstorming ideas with you and having your logical view of things has been beneficial.

To Brian Degenstien, my colleague and friend, your ideas about me getting away from all the distractions so I could write helped me finish this book so much sooner.

To the Reverend Dr. Danielle James. Our debates illuminated the good and the bad. For that education I am thankful. Your friendship is missed.

To Brenda Robinson, my editor. Your thoughts clarified mine – and your math skills are impressive too!

To Bruce Serbin, my publicist. Your patience with my eight million emails and my scientifically erratic creative process was epic. This book would not be what it is without your input.

To Dawn Andrews Siebold, all your feedback to my endless logistics questions, and even more importantly, your enthusiasm and candid support is appreciated. You always help make things easier.

And last but definitely not least, to Steve Siebold, my speaking mentor. Truly, without you, Success through Manipulation would not exist.

Foreword

By Steve Siebold.

Colin Christopher offers a fresh perspective to personal development and mind manipulation. As a world-class clinical hypnotherapist, he shares the unequaled power of the subconscious mind in a way that is certain to shake the rafters of conventional self-help wisdom.

This book breaks down the mental laws one by one and offers a clear and concise understanding of a complex and often confusing subject.

Whether you wish to earn more money, get in shape or enjoy more enriching relationships, this book will detail the subconscious strategy required to turn your dreams into reality.

Don't let the word manipulation turn you off. The truth is we are all being mentally and emotionally manipulated every day of our lives, sometimes by others and more often by ourselves. Some of this manipulation serves our best interests; such as the emotional self-manipulation of motivating ourselves to stick to a budget, exercise more or eat less. Just as often we experience negative manipulation that holds us back and keeps us from realizing our own potential.

The difference lies in understanding the mind mechanics behind the manipulation and directing that knowledge to help us become our best selves.

This book takes you behind the scenes and dissects the laws that create both positive and negative results. Colin explains these laws in easy to follow, layman's terms that anyone can follow and immediately put into practice. As you read and study these laws you will find yourself both shocked and surprised at their simplicity and at the personal and professional impact of fully understanding them.

Most personal development books repeat the same principles over and over, but Success Through Manipulation cuts through the clutter and elevates self-help to a new level. This is Psycho-Cybernetics for the 21st century.

As a successful author and professional speaker, I have a backstage pass to the best of the best in the industry, and Colin Christopher was the first person I called when a family member was experiencing trouble relaxing and sleeping. Within days the problem began to dissipate and a few months later it had completely disappeared.

Colin understands mind manipulation at a higher level than anyone I've ever seen, and his extensive knowledge is carefully detailed in this book.

Study his work, set your goals and get ready for the best results of your life!

Steve Siebold
Author, How Rich People Think
December 25, 2012

Contents

Part III – Social Dynamics – How Your Mind Works With Others 159

Introduction

Your thinking is being manipulated right now, whether you know it or not. Manipulation is everywhere, and it is affecting you, no matter what level of success you currently enjoy.

Do you realize you are being manipulated, or are you oblivious? Do you know who or what is manipulating you? Can you identify the manipulation? If you can identify it, can you do anything about it? How is manipulation affecting you? Can you change these effects? Can you use them to your advantage?

As a hypnotist, I routinely use thought manipulation. On stage, I use it to entertain. One-on-one, I use it to help clients.

How can thought manipulation create more success?

Let me give you an example. Think of a brain surgeon. To save a life, the surgeon manipulates physical tools to remove a tumour from the patient's brain. As a hypnotist on stage, I'm like that surgeon; but I manipulate mental tools to get inside the minds of volunteers to change how they think about themselves.

In general, these volunteers are afraid of being on stage and worried about embarrassing themselves. Despite these mental obstacles, in a matter of minutes, I manipulate their thinking so they can do unbelievable things in front of hundreds of people despite their fears. I do one routine where they think they're driving a race car, crash into a deer, and save the deer's life with mouth-to-mouth resuscitation. Picture that!

In private practice as a clinical hypnotherapist, I've used these same thought manipulation tools to help people lose weight, quit smoking, break bad habits, improve self-confidence, eliminate fears and phobias, heighten sexual performance, increase the quality of athletic performance, improve study and concentration skills, and just plain improvement of personal and work performance in general.

If these mental tools can manipulate someone's thinking like that, they can certainly be used to manipulate your thinking to help you become more successful.

These mental tools can be broken down into individual components that produce specific results in response to thoughts, beliefs and habits. The individual components of these mental tools are called "The Laws of Manipulation." Whether you are aware of these laws or not, they are affecting you right now because you constantly have thoughts, beliefs and habits that fit into the laws directly.

When you keep the same thoughts, beliefs and habits, the Laws of Manipulation create the same outcomes. To change these outcomes, you have to change your thoughts, beliefs and habits so the laws can create new results. In essence, think differently and you change your results... and your life.

So how should you change your thinking? That's up to you, but it makes sense to think, believe and act like highly successful people. This way, the Laws of Manipulation can work for you and affect your results in the same way they do for highly successful people.

So what do highly successful people think? We know they think differently. But how do they think differently compared to poor or average achievers? This difference in thinking is what the Success through Manipulation process reveals. At the same time, it also gives you tools for fostering the change you desire.
In the Success through Manipulation process, the difference in thinking between poor to average achievers and highly successful performers is referred to as "conventional thinking" versus "unconventional thinking."

Conventional thinking refers to the way poor to average performers think. Conventional thinking is predictable and results from instinctual reaction to environment, people and what is deemed socially acceptable.

Unconventional thinking refers to the way highly successful performers think. Unconventional thinking is analytical, proactive and based on conscious evaluation of environment and people.

I use these references throughout this book to make the distinction between the poor to average performers (conventional thinkers) and highly successful performers (unconventional thinkers). The Laws of Manipulation create different results based on these differences in thinking.

I'll give you a quick example:

When you first picked up this book, what was your thinking about manipulation? Take a second and remember.

In my experience, most people automatically think about manipulation negatively. Conventional thinkers say manipulation is bad.

Unconventional thinkers analyze manipulation and say the word itself isn't what's bad. It's the outcome of manipulation that's positive or negative.

When you're driving, you manipulate the steering wheel to get to where you're going. Manipulate poorly, you crash. Manipulate like a world-class race car driver, and you could win the Indy 500. Unconventional thinkers say manipulation is the action you take. How you use manipulation to achieve a specific outcome is what's positive or negative.

When you were first thinking about manipulation, was it based on conventional or unconventional thinking?

If you find yourself saying, "Not all successful people think like that or do that," you are correct. My comparisons are based on my experience as a clinical hypnotherapist on stage and in private sessions with clients. There I have observed differences in thinking between successful performers and poor to average performers with bad habits, afflictions, and performance issues.

Based on my observations, it's obvious there is a huge gap between these performance levels. That gap is a direct result of the laws of manipulation producing different results in response to differences in thinking. If you want to be more successful, it's time to choose to think like a highly successful performer so the Laws of Manipulation can create better results in your life and increase your level of success.

Choosing to change your thinking can be a difficult process. The Laws of Manipulation themselves are tools that you can use to aid you in the process of changing your thinking.

Each chapter of this book covers a specific Law of Manipulation. The chapters will do the following:

1)   Define the law.
2)   Where necessary, give background information or common examples to help further your understanding of the law.
3)   Discuss how conventional and unconventional thinkers react to and/or use the law.
4)   Provide thought manipulation action steps you can take to critically apply the law to your own situation and change your thinking.

Success through Manipulation is not an easy choice. You won't agree with everything. That's good because not agreeing is a trait of many high achieving successful people. I wish you luck and great success!

Visit my website and let me know how your success is progressing.

http://www.successthroughmanipulation.com

I wish you great success!

Colin Christopher
Juneau, Alaska, United States
August 29, 2012

Part I
– The Fundamentals –
How Your Mind Works

1
The Law of Subconscious Habits

Definition

The subconscious mind responds automatically to a real or imagined environment. These responses become programmed into the subconscious mind and form habits.

Background Information

The subconscious mind is an automatic response storehouse like the hard drive in a computer. It remembers its responses to stimuli that come from instincts and learned experiences. It processes 20 million environmental stimuli per second and responds habitually to what it processes without the awareness of the conscious mind. This is much like you sitting at a computer and typing. You are consciously aware of what you are typing, but you are unaware of the thousands of processes going on inside your computer and being stored on the hard drive.

The subconscious mind only perceives and makes decisions in the present and is strictly habitual. Because it is habitual, the subconscious mind will produce the same behavioural responses to the same stimuli unless altered with new learned experiences.

For example, going back to the computer, your hard drive has different programs on it that tell the computer to do things in a certain way. Unless the programming changes, it will do the same thing every time because that's what it is programmed to do.

In the subconscious mind, environmental stimulus and learned experiences can either be real or imaged. Whether real or imagined, the subconscious does not know the difference between the real and the imagined. It perceives both as real and responds accordingly. Therefore, what you think about and imagine programs your subconscious habits just as much as real world experience.

A great book that illustrates all of this in depth along with reference to all the scientific research is The Biology of Belief by Dr. Bruce Lipton.

Example

Think about tying your shoelaces. When you first learned how to do this, you put in lots of conscious attention. But think about it. When was the last time you thought about how to tie your shoelaces? Once you learned how, your subconscious was programmed to do it automatically. It became habit, and this habit gives you the freedom to concentrate on other things.

Think about driving. To learn to drive, you put in a great deal of concentration, but once you learned it, it became a habit. You could consciously focus on other things like holding a conversation with a passenger or thinking about your day or navigating the road without crashing into other cars and trees.

The previous two examples illustrate real stimuli that your subconscious habitually responds to. But what about imagined stimuli? Think about yourself sitting in a movie theatre watching a scary movie. There is no physical danger, and yet your teeth clench, you feel nauseated, and scared watching the movie! This real feeling of fear is a subconscious, habitual response created in reaction to the horror movie. Your subconscious responds to the imagined danger in the movie and causes real physical responses in your body.

Discussion

Conventional thinkers generally spend the majority of their time performing the same habitual behaviours. They let the decisions and programming they put into their subconscious mind in the past control the majority of their life. Their formative years are long since past. Unless there is a major upheaval, they rarely change because there are very few new learned experiences (or none at all) that result in subconscious programming that creates behavioural response shifts.

When viewed objectively, conventional thinkers appear to be followers. They are slaves to their habits, and this makes them seem drone-like.

Unconventional thinkers are usually leaders and creators because they spend their time gaining new experiences through physical, mental, emotional and/or spiritual personal development. Based on this development, their thinking evolves and changes over time. This evolution and change provides new programming for their subconscious minds. This new programming produces new habits that create different results.

Thought Manipulation Action Step for Today

Identify your habits. What have you learned to do that you no longer think about but just do automatically, starting with getting up, brushing your teeth, driving your car, going on coffee breaks, checking Facebook and Twitter (or email, websites and other social media), exercising, preparing food etc.? List good habits and bad ones.

What portion of your day is spent performing habitual behaviours and what portion is spent learning new experiences? What's the ratio of time spent? Is this ratio keeping you in the drone zone or is it helping you evolve and improve?

Change the ratio of your time spent between performing habitual behaviours and learning from new experiences, and observe the results. Then adjust accordingly based on your observations.

2
The Law of Conscious Interpretation

Definition

The conscious mind interprets a real or imagined environment and makes decisions based on what it understands.

Background Information

Unlike the subconscious mind that only perceives and makes decisions in the present, the conscious mind is the awareness you have to think in past, present and/or future terms. This allows you to make critical decisions and be spontaneously creative in response to your real or imagined environment. Where the subconscious mind is AUTOMATIC control that PROCESSES 20 million environmental stimuli per second, the conscious mind is MANUAL Control that INTERPRETS only 40 environmental stimuli per second (Lipton, The Biology of Belief, 2005). Yes you read that right: 20,000,000 versus 40.

Where the subconscious mind processes overwhelming amounts of information automatically, the conscious mind focuses on much less information so it can interpret and generate new responses. These new responses are the cornerstones for improvement and change.

Again if you think of the subconscious mind as a computer hard drive operating in the background responding to the millions of lines of computer code it takes to run your computer, you can think of the conscious mind as you sitting at that computer typing with the keyboard. You can only type so fast while the computer processes everything else in the background.

Example

Think about when you were in school. You learned to make decisions based on how you interpret the knowledge that teachers and books gave you.

Think about when you are experiencing something new. Your conscious mind makes the decision to like or dislike the new experience. Based on your decision, you decide whether or not to participate again in the future.

Let's take driving again. Assuming you know how to drive in North America, and you get on a plane to England. You get there, rent a car and start driving.

You know how to drive, but there are three important differences. An unfamiliar place, the driver's side is now the passenger side, and you drive on the opposite side of the road.

Your subconscious habitual response is to drive like you're in North America. Most likely it's awkward to make such drastic changes that go against your habit to drive on the right side of the road. Your conscious interprets the new information of driving on the left in a new country on what feels like the passenger side.

As your conscious mind focuses and interprets the new way of driving, it decides on new behaviour that is appropriate for the situation. This is based on the new experience interpreted with knowledge of your past experiences. While this is happening your subconscious mind records the entire experience and records the interpreted new behavioural responses generated by the conscious mind. This way your subconscious mind can respond the same way in the future based on your new decisions to drive in England.

Discussion

Conventional thinkers spend little time making conscious decisions. They spend much of their time doing conventional repetitive tasks that require little to no thinking or decision-making. The repetitive tasks they perform may have originally been challenging, but they've been repeated for so long they no longer require conscious thought. In the absence of conscious decision making and constructive action, conventional thinkers spend their time complaining about how bad things are and offer no real useful insight on how to improve a situation or a problem. If they do have insight, they lack the drive to take action. The conventional thinker bases most decisions on past experience and subconscious habitual responses without taking into account much new information. They are usually satisfied with keeping the status quo.

Unconventional thinkers spend more time learning, thinking, gathering new information and then applying that information to current situations and new problems. They spend time coming up with creative solutions and they spend more time creating. Their decisions are based on new learning or the acquisition of new experiences and knowledge to create wisdom. They apply this wisdom to override or compliment their current subconscious habitual responses. They like trying and doing new things.

Thought Manipulation Action Step for Today

Identify the last time you used new information that resulted in making a conscious decision.

How much of that decision was based on prior experience and memories and how much of that decision was based on new information?

Was the decision affected by your subconscious habitual responses or affected strictly by conscious interpretation?

Think about how many decisions you make on a daily basis and decide which ones are primarily affected by your subconscious habitual responses and how many are affected by conscious interpretation.

Decide what action(s) you will perform to change the amount of influence your conscious interpretation has on your decision-making and then execute these actions.

3
The Law of Brain Waves

Definition

Brain wave states can be changed to aid learning and direct subconscious programming.

Background Information

There are five brain wave states defined and measured by electroencephalograms (EEGs). Each state is associated with different brain activity.

Delta – 0.5 to 4 Hz (cycles per second) – Associated with sleep and the predominant brain wave activity of babies.

Theta – 4 to 8 Hz – Associated with a light sleep and/or children 2 to 6 years of age.

Alpha – 8 to 12 Hz – Associated with calm consciousness and an awareness of self.

Beta – 12 to 35 Hz – Associated with active focused consciousness, such as thinking, reading, and interpreting.

Gamma – **Greater than 35 Hz** – Associated with states of peak performance, such as when a pilot is landing a plane.

Delta and Theta states are the brain wave states where people are the most suggestive and programmable. It's no coincidence that from birth to age 6 (the formative years), children are in these brain wave states so they can observe (with all of their senses and emotions) and record into their subconscious all the environmental stimulus, beliefs, behaviours, and language(s) etc., around them. (Lipton, The Biology of Belief, 2005).

People are more suggestible and programmable in these lower brain wave states, and as a hypnotist I take advantage of these lowered states to reprogram the subconscious minds of my clients and volunteers on stage.

Example

Brain waves are actually very easy to alter and you do it all the time without much thought, from going to sleep to waking up and going about your day. They alter based on the activity you are doing and the amount of focus, concentration, and interpretation you are participating in.

Do a quick search on Google and you'll see (depending on the study) the average American watches between 4 and 8 hours of TV a day.

EEG readings show low brain wave activity while watching TV, so there isn't a lot of interpretation and decision-making going on while staring at the screen. This lowered brain wave activity makes you more suggestible and programmable.

Changing emotional states changes brain waves.

Brain waves change when using mind altering substances, such as drugs and alcohol.

Discussion

Conventional thinkers aren't usually aware of their brain waves and neither are unconventional thinkers. It's not something people think about.

Conventional thinkers spend much of their time allowing themselves to be in lower brain wave states (watching TV, etc.) and spend this time being programmed by their surroundings and accept the influence their surroundings provide. Instead of operating at peak performance whenever possible, they do the bare minimum to get by and so their brain waves are never pushed to their upper limits.

Unconventional thinkers, whether they are aware of their brain wave states or not, spend more time changing their brain wave states from higher (performing intense thought activity) to lower (meditation and other brain wave calming techniques) and vice versa. They operate in peak performance mode and intentionally challenge their minds much more often. While their minds are challenged, their brain waves are in higher states and they are able to concentrate and focus more easily, more of the time. They may even receive a thrill from heightened concentration levels. To balance their peak performance they seek times of rest or distraction, where their minds are inspired. During these times of rest or distraction, unconventional thinkers select activities that program their brains with something desirable. They may watch TV, but the content is educational versus escapist to pass the time. Where possible, they choose surroundings that allow their brains to be and feel inspired.

Thought Manipulation Action Step for Today

Purposely pick two constructive activities, one to lower and then one to raise your brain wave state for 10 to 15 minutes. Meditation works well for lowering and for raising brave wave states. Try an activity that requires intense focus, like learning to juggle or reading Shakespeare or other literature you find challenging.

Afterwards notice the differences in how you feel when you lower and raise your brain wave states intentionally.

Examine your daily routine. How have you been lowering or increasing your brain wave states, whether on purpose or by accident?

When you do change your brain wave state (especially when you're lowering them, in cases like watching TV), what are your surroundings programming into your mind?

Is the programming you're putting into your subconscious constructive and useful or is it detrimental?

Is the way you're altering your brain waves constructive or destructive (such as when using alcohol or drugs) to your physical body? If it is destructive, decide on an action to take to eliminate destructive brain wave alteration. If it is constructive, decide on an action to amplify it, such as increasing the length of time where your brain wave state is higher.

4
The Law of the Gatekeeper

Definition

The conscious mind is the gatekeeper of the subconscious mind. Any time the conscious mind is impaired, distracted, unconscious, or focused on something intently, the conscious mind's function as the gatekeeper is rendered ineffective and the subconscious mind can be programmed.

Background Information

The conscious mind keeps the subconscious mind from receiving new programming that would create new (or change existing) subconscious habitual responses. Some of the time the gatekeeper is desirable because you don't want random environmental stimuli and thought bombardment to influence you. Other times you don't want the wrong people influencing you.

Some of the time the gatekeeper is detrimental by keeping you from creating or modify your existing subconscious habitual responses. For example, there are times you want to do something differently, but your conscious mind just won't let you. This is because what you desire to do differently seems opposed to your current thoughts, beliefs, and habits. The gatekeeper just doesn't let new programming in.

Example

Hypnosis is an excellent example of deliberate intent to bypass your critical faculties. Putting a subject into a relaxed state of mind does this. When relaxed, brain wave states lower, making the subconscious mind more receptive to programming, and your conscious mind is distracted by the relaxation, and the gatekeeper can be bypassed.

Other times when your conscious is impaired or distracted are when you are under the influence of alcohol or drugs. It's not uncommon in the business world to ply potential buyers with alcohol to make them more malleable and receptive to the influence of the seller.

When you are sleeping or unconscious, your subconscious mind is still receiving input from your five senses and your subconscious is susceptible to any programming your five senses deliver.

Magnetic and electromagnetic fields, emitted from fridges, stoves, alarm clocks, TVs, cell phones, computers, power lines, and other electronic units can alter brain chemistry. It is now unclear how much this alteration in brain chemistry affects people's conscious and subconscious minds. However, it is something to be aware of and, if you choose, err on the side of caution when you can to limit your exposure.

Other times the conscious mind is impaired, distracted, or focused on something intently are during times of extreme physical pain, shock, intense emotion, torture, brainwashing, watching TV, playing video games, listening to music, and more.

Discussion

Conventional thinkers have their gatekeeper engaged almost constantly. They feel better when everything and everyone around them conform to their expectations and beliefs. In extreme cases it's very hard for them to relax, and they are so stressed from overworking their gatekeeper, they eventually burn out. In management situations, they become the micromanager.

When new opportunities and ideas that could be beneficial occur, they miss out because their gatekeeper is protecting and controlling everything. During times when the conventional thinker truly wishes to allow new ideas and opportunities to come to them, they find it very difficult to let go of the thinking, beliefs and habits they currently have. They say, "Change is too hard." They're deluding themselves because change isn't really the hard part for them, letting go of their control and limiting beliefs is what is hard. Their control and beliefs feel comfortable, and they want to hold onto that comfortable feeling. Even if the change is beneficial, the feeling of comfort is more important to them.

In extreme cases, when their conscious mind is finally distracted or impaired, the conventional thinker breaks down and vast amounts of emotions rush out and are vented. This happens in the hypnotherapy chair with clients massively crying to the point of shrieking and wailing.

Unconventional thinkers allow time and space for their conscious minds to be distracted – often several times a day. When required, they trust their gatekeeper to ward off the obvious influence of negative ideas and environmental stimulus that create subconscious programming in opposition to their success. However, whenever they do rest their gatekeeper, they consciously remove influences they believe to be detrimental. They make sure they are doing something or are surrounded by environmental stimulus that they perceive to be beneficial. The kinds of stimulus they prefer offer new ideas and information that can impress their subconscious minds once they begin the gatekeeper rest period. Activities can include meditation, watching educational programs, or even talking to a friend on the phone.

Thought Manipulation Action Step for Today

Ask yourself if you find it more comfortable to constantly be in control because you believe your way is the right way? Or are you comfortable letting go and allowing others to do and say what they believe so you can focus on being successful?
How often do you find yourself letting go and just relaxing in the presence

of beneficial stimulus that can impress your subconscious mind? Choose one way to do this at least once a day (three to six times would be better) for five to 15 minutes.

Part I
Final Note

These first four laws form the basis for hypnosis and Success through Manipulation. Hypnosis is a process where a subject (either through guidance from someone else like a hypnotherapist, or through their own self guidance) begins to focus on relaxation.

The relaxation is not necessary, however it serves four purposes:

1) Gives the conscious mind something to focus on so it becomes distracted and its gatekeeper function can effectively be bypassed.
2) Allows direct access to the thinking, ideas, beliefs and habits, currently programmed in the subconscious mind (through the distraction of the gatekeeper).
3) Provides a safe comfortable environment for exploring and analyzing current and new thinking, ideas, beliefs, and habits.
4) Lowers the brain wave state of the subject to facilitate new programming of the subconscious mind and substantially speed up the change process.

The Success through Manipulation process operates the same way. Each of the Laws of Manipulation in this book serve to provide you with ways to directly access the programming of your subconscious mind so you can safely explore and analyze your thinking, ideas, beliefs and habits and program/reprogram your subconscious mind with new thinking, ideas, beliefs, and habits that will make you more successful.

Part II
Internal Dynamics
How Your Mind Works
With Itself

5
The Law of Language Translation

Definition

The dominant form of communication for the subconscious mind is language that is easily translated into pictures. Any words the subconscious cannot translate into pictures are ignored.

Background Information

The conscious mind understands complex communication, and this allows it to understand words that aren't easily interpreted into images. With this ability to understand, ideas can be communicated and understood in the form of language.

The subconscious mind does not understand complex language communication. It receives input from your five senses, and these senses do not include a language sense. As such, the subconscious responds to communication that is translated into your five senses. Your visual sense is the primary translation facilitator for communication, and anything that cannot be seen as a picture by the subconscious is ignored (for the purpose of communication).

To understand this, think of yourself in a foreign country where you do not know the language. In a restaurant, to communicate what you want to eat, you would point to a picture on the menu of the food you desire, or point to another person's meal that looks appealing. Any idea that can be communicated visually (translated into a picture) is easily understood by the subconscious mind. This is how your subconscious operates all the time – using your visual sense.

The old cliché "A picture is worth a thousand words" is true. Magazines and comic books are very easy to understand because ideas are broken down into images.

Apple Inc. under Steve Jobs was excellent at creating products that took advantage of images and pictures and made complex ideas simple. Enter the iPad, iPhone, etc.

Every complex man-made object from a skyscraper to a space shuttle started off as an image (blueprints).

Images really are the universal language and are one of the most useful forms of communication from primitive cave drawings to the Mona Lisa. They are a powerful means to communicate ideas. Picture a purple penguin. What did you see in your mind?

There is much that can be said to illustrate the translation of language to the subconscious regarding the other four senses. But for the purposes of this specific law, images are the primary means of conscious communication to program the subconscious mind.

Reducing a complex idea to an image or a series of images is the fastest and easiest way to have a complex idea impressed on the subconscious and program it with new information. This will be covered in a greater extent in The Law of Visualization.

Example

When a smoker says, "I will quit smoking," what is the predominant image? What does a picture of quitting smoking look like? A circle with a line crossing out a cigarette is the universal sign for no smoking. But there is still an image of a cigarette in that picture.

The word "quit" does not readily translate into a picture in the subconscious, only the word "smoking" can easily translate into a picture, and the focus becomes "smoking." Since the picture of a cigarette is easily translated, the subconscious perceives that the conscious mind is communicating that it wants to smoke.

The subconscious will respond directly to the images that are received and programmed into it. To change the image the subconscious receives, instead of saying, "I will quit smoking," say, "I will breathe clean, fresh air." That is a completely different image and a completely different focus communicated to the subconscious. Continually focusing on breathing clean fresh air programs the subconscious to breathe clean fresh air, and it will respond accordingly.

Discussion

Conventional thinkers are bad to mediocre communicators with other people and with their own subconscious. This has nothing to do with intelligence; they can be some of the smartest people you know. They just have difficulty (for a multitude of reasons) communicating ideas in a form that is easily understood in image form. Many (not all) conventional thinkers are unaware of the effect image programming has on their subconscious. Again, they spend their time watching TV and playing video games. Their lack of conscious awareness of what is happening allows these activities to program their subconscious with the images that are on the TV or a video game. Because they lack conscious awareness of image communication, other people's images program their subconscious.

Keep in mind there is a difference between watching TV for inspiration, education, or distraction to allow the conscious mind to rest versus watching it to pass the time. Because there is a different intent, the content of what is being watched is usually different. Content that is educational or inspirational can program the subconscious with images that are beneficial.

Unconventional thinkers can break down complex ideas and express them in language that is easy to translate into images, so internal understanding (themselves) and external (other people) understanding can take place. This makes them excellent communicators. If language can't be broken down into a single image, they break it down into a series of images that communicate a complex idea. The images they create program their subconscious.

Thought Manipulation Action Step for Today

Identify a complex idea or thought you want to communicate to someone else or a group of people. When you are communicating this idea or thought, does the language you use translate easily into images that you and other people can easily understand and identify?

Can you take the complex idea you are thinking of or working on and translate it into an image? If not, can you break down the complex ideas into a series of images?

Look at the people you like and dislike. Does the language they use translate easily to images? Do you like people more when they communicate effectively or do you like them less?

How much time in an average week are you letting outside images created by others influence you?

How much time in an average week are you actively performing activities, such as reading or listening to audio or watching videos that stimulate your mind with new ideas that create new images for your conscious and subconscious mind to interpret and process for creativity?

6
The Law of Opposite Language

Definition

In the subconscious mind, words that are meant to communicate the opposite of a described image (like "not" or "don't" or "can't") are translated into the image you are referring to. This creates the opposite meaning that is intended to be consciously communicated, and the intended meaning is ignored subconsciously.

Background Information

As language is translated into its image equivalent, words like "not" and "don't" are lost because they are meant to communicate the absence (or opposite) of something. However, this absence is actually of the thing that it is present.

As described in The Law of Language Translation, language will always have an image focus for the subconscious. If there is no image focus, communication will not be perceived by the subconscious. The conscious mind will interpret the negative directly opposite of the way it was intended, and the subconscious perceives it the way the image is represented. This creates incongruity in communication between the subconscious and the conscious. When incongruity occurs, the image focus of the subconscious mind is dominant, and the subconscious will work towards making the image become reality.

Example

When I say, "Don't think of a cow," the first image that comes to mind is of a cow. Depending on your ability to visualize, you may have been able to think of something else consciously, but for a split second your brain converted the language into an image of a cow, and that is what your subconscious mind perceived.

Don't drink and drive. When sober, this makes complete sense to the conscious mind. Unfortunately the picture focus is drink and drive. When under the influence of alcohol, the conscious mind is bypassed and subconscious habitual response takes over. The image focus "Drink and Drive" reinforced with advertising everywhere while conscious is automatically followed. The subconscious says drink and drive because that's what the image has programmed it to do. Thankfully, I've seen many ads over the last few years saying, "Drive Safe and Drive Sober" and "Arrive Alive, Drive Sober." In the conscious mind, they are interpreted to mean don't drink and drive, but they program the subconscious mind differently and have a greater probability of generating a different action when subconscious habitual response takes over in an impaired state.

Children are great at illustrating this. How many times do you hear parents say, "Don't do that!" "Don't run." "Don't hit your brother/sister." It's only when the child is frightened by an angry parent yelling, "Why don't you listen to me," that the child finally listens. There are two factors at work here:

1) While the child is being frightened by the angry screaming parent, they are in a highly suggestible state where the conscious mind is bypassed (see The Law of the Gate Keeper) and the subconscious is directly open to programming. Their subconscious creates a new subconscious habitual response with the image focus of "Listen to me." This image focus is becomes associated and triggered by parental anger. So programmed in a frightened state, the child suddenly listens.

2) A new subconscious habitual response is also created in the angry parent. It that says their child will only listen to them when the parent is angry. This scenario plays out over and over because of "not" language.

By the time kids are teens, parents are always wondering why their kids don't listen to them until they are angry. It's because they programmed their kids to not listen to them until they're angry when they were little, and this programming is habit. There are of course other reasons, but this is a major contributing factor. It can help your relationships by changing your opposite language.

Discussion

Conventional thinkers tend to express themselves in a "not" way. They're always saying or complaining about what they "don't want to happen." "I don't want this." "I don't want that." "Don't do that." The problem with expressing themselves in not language is the image focus of their language is usually the opposite of what they want. This image focus is programmed into their subconscious and then their subconscious automatically gives them what they don't want.

Unconventional Thinkers express themselves in terms of images. Their language creates a focus on what they actually want. When they do express themselves in not language, their focus is still on what they do want.

For example, when a child is crying the conventional thinker says, "Why are you crying? Don't cry." The unconventional thinker takes advantage of not language, smiles at the child and says, "I see you're not smiling. Why are you not smiling?" Because the child is in an emotional state their gatekeeper is bypassed and their subconscious is programmed with the image focus of smiling and very quickly the crying child begins to smile. I spent years working with troubled children and teens and this works exceptionally well when done properly.

Thought Manipulation Action Step for Today

Observe how others speak today and notice their opposite language.

Observe how you speak today. How many times a day do you use opposite language? If it's difficult for you to notice your opposite language, ask a friend/co-worker to pay attention to it for you and tell you how often you do it.

Determine what you are saying to yourself and to other people that use opposite language. Does what you say create or reinforce images that are different from what you want to communicate?

Determine what things you are saying to yourself (and to other people who use opposite language) that reinforces your focus on what you want.

Many people realize how much opposite language affects their thinking and become frustrated. They find they constantly catch themselves. Realize you've been doing it automatically, possibly for your whole life. It will take some time to change. Have a little fun with it. Say, "I will not use 'not' language that creates mental images of what I don't want." Reread that sentence, taking out the opposites/negatives "not" and "don't." The message focus becomes "I will use language that creates mental images of what I want."

7
The Law of Triggers

Definition

A specific situation, feeling, or event causes a reaction every time that same situation, feeling or event occurs.

Example

Think about being in bed. Your partner starts snoring and you really want to get some sleep. Their snoring keeps you awake, and you feel very annoyed and angry with them. In fact, every time they snore from that point on, it triggers your feelings of being annoyed and angry.

Think about being at work. Your boss has a negative attitude. When you speak with him, his negative attitude triggers you to think negatively, and you have a bad day. Then you get home and you sit down with your pet. Your love for your pet triggers positive feelings, and your attitude shifts.

Think about your relationship with your parents or other authority figures. When you were young, you were told what to do and had to follow their rules. When you did not agree with their decisions, this created stress and resentment. As an adult, when people in authority tell you what to do, despite your own better judgement, stress and resentment is triggered.

Discussion

Conventional thinkers want to take control of the stimulus that triggers them. If triggers produce negative reactions, they attempt to get rid of the stimulus that sets off the trigger(s) or remove themselves from that stimulus. If stimulus triggers positive reactions, they want to maintain that stimulus. This makes the success of the conventional thinker dependent on the presence or absence of stimulus, and presents two problems:

1) When stimulus that triggers negative results reappears, it again produces negative results.
2) When stimulus that triggers positive results is removed, positive results disappear.

Unconventional thinkers monitor their thoughts in the presence or absence of stimulus that triggers them. Monitoring their thoughts allows them to objectively monitor their triggered responses to the stimulus. By monitoring and then changing their thoughts based on their observations, the stimulus can no longer trigger the same reaction it did before. This makes the unconventional thinker's success dependent on his or her own thinking. Their success is independent of the stimulus the conventional thinker either avoids or becomes dependent on.

Thought Manipulation Action Step for Today

Examine areas where stimulus is triggering you into specific results (both negative and positive).

For each trigger, ask yourself:

1) What am I thinking when stimulus activates this trigger?
2) How is this affecting my results?
3) What results do I really want to have?
4) Is my achievement of these results dependent on the presence or absence of this stimulus?

Take responsibility and decide how you want to change your thinking so your result is dependent on your thinking.

8
The Law of Association

Definition

In the presence of a trigger event, a thought/action that creates a specific result links the trigger, thought/action and result together. These links become a subconscious habit where even if the thought/action is removed, the trigger event still produces the same specific result.

Background Information

You may remember learning about Pavlov's dog in school. Essentially Ivan Pavlov created training where he rang a bell at meal times, causing a dog to expect food and salivate. Over time, Pavlov removed the food and only rang the bell. For the dog, the ringing bell was linked with food and caused salivating. When there was no food, the ringing bell still made the dog salivate. An association between the bell, salivation, and food was created.

Example

Think about a smoker. A smoker tends to crave a cigarette when drinking their morning coffee or an adult drink with friends that smoke. When a smoker tries to quit smoking, he still has morning coffee or a drink with other smokers. Just as Pavlov took away the food from his dog, a smoker trying to quit takes away his cigarettes. Still coffee and drinks with friends trigger a desire to smoke.

Discussion

Conventional thinkers allow the formation of bad habits by letting their emotions react to environmental stimulus, such as stress, failure, social rejection, and repeated negative thinking. These environmental stimuli create chain reactions that trigger observable outcomes, including burnout, low self-esteem, familial fighting and so forth.

To cope with these negative outcomes, over time conventional thinkers try to escape through distractions. Distractions come in many forms, and some can be constructive. However, many are destructive, like smoking, overeating, drinking, drug use, sex addiction, gambling, alcoholism and more.

Like Pavlov's bell, a link occurs over time between the following elements: 1) The repeated distractions, 2) The environmental stimulus causing stress, and 3) The observable outcomes. These associations create a vicious cycle — each element reinforces the other, and escape from the bad habit seems impossible.

For example, the low performer experiences a lack of success, and then feels bad. To cope, an escape is sought to alleviate that bad feeling. Escape takes many forms, but usually it's a bad habit. The escape is fleeting and any momentary alleviation of feeling bad is diminished. That's because the escape is associated with being unsuccessful and feeling bad.

Unconventional thinkers allow the formation of good habits by examining how they feel and making the decision to feel good. No matter what the environmental stimulus is, they decide to feel good. Because they dictate how they feel instead of letting their emotions react to environmental stimulus, unconventional thinkers do not have the desire to find an escape. Instead, feeling good results in unshakable self-confidence in their abilities, and this in turn keeps unconventional thinkers from developing bad habits. Because they feel good, and their self-confidence is high, they spend their time finding ways to create success in their lives no matter what the environmental conditions are.

Over time, connections are created between the elements of self-confidence, feeling good, and success. This creates a powerful associated conditioned response. In highly successful people these associations are so powerful, only one of the three elements is required to produce the others.

When Donald Trump lost his fortune for the first time, his success and his feeling good were lost. His powerful self-confidence and his constant thoughts about success (instead of his losses) recreated his fortune and his good feelings. His great success is an associated conditioned response to his desire to feel good and his high self-confidence.

Thought Manipulation Action Step for Today

Examine your habits (the good and the bad) and identify the following four elements that may repeatedly be present as you perform your habit:

1) Your thoughts
2) Your actions
3) Your feelings
4) Environmental stimulus

Think of these four elements individually as four different Pavlovian bells.

Now duplicate each of the four elements individually by ringing each bell separately and observing the results. Notice the strength or weakness of your desire to perform your habit when you duplicate each element. The stronger the desire, the more powerful the association between the habit and the individual element.

To create positive associations that become good habits, start by thinking about small outcomes of success you desire and begin thinking these thoughts whenever you feel good. Make a conscious effort to feel good no matter what. With each small success your self-confidence will increase. As you succeed in small things, your good feelings will associate themselves with your successes and your self-confidence will soar. Then with the links created, start thinking about bigger successful outcomes or results. Forming these associations usually takes anywhere between one to three weeks, depending on the individual. You may or may not find this easy. No matter how much work it takes, it is your responsibility to think about success and make sure you learn to feel good while you're doing it, no matter what.

To remove negative associations and bad habits, you need to discover what triggers your bad habits by doing the examination of the four elements described above. With this awareness, revisit the Law of Triggers in the last chapter and make your results dependent on how you think, instead of on the presence or absence of triggers.

9
The Law of Fight or Flight

Definition

Self-preservation is the dominant instinct in response to real or perceived danger, and it takes precedence over all other responses.

Background Information

When your wellbeing is threatened by real or imagined danger, your instinctual flight or fight response creates fear. There is a cascade of physical, mental, emotional, and biochemical reactions that prepares your body to run away or to fight. The purpose of these responses is to help you avoid danger and/or physically fight to survive.

During the time of the real or perceived danger, your conscious interpretation is bypassed because of intense biochemical reactions. While your conscious interpretation is bypassed, your primal subconscious habits for survival are triggered and become very difficult to overcome or control with rational thought. (Lipton, Biology of Belief, 2005).

Example

In today's modern society, there are few real physical danger scenarios where flight or flight can be triggered. It's unlikely any of us is going to be hunted and eaten by a lion anytime soon. However physical scenarios like being mugged or attacked do happen. In situations where real danger exists, fight or flight is a useful survival mechanism.

In today's world, we are much more likely to be exposed to perceptions of danger (imagined danger). Women and men can perceive danger walking home late at night, even when there is no danger at all. Turbulence on an airplane makes many travelers fearful because they believe they are out of control and are going to crash.

Other ways fear can be triggered are from stress at work or at home and sometimes even driving in traffic. Watching scary movies can do it. Agoraphobia (the fear of open spaces) is a great example. There is no physical danger associated with open spaces, however the fight or flight response is triggered creating anxiety. Any scenario you can think of where no real danger exists but danger is perceived can trigger a fight or flight response.

Salespeople (especially new ones) fear rejection by the customer. Their emotional reaction can be so overwhelming that it causes doubt, self-pity, lack of self-confidence, and in some cases even pain. Not being accepted for any reason can create fear in many people. There is no physical danger yet fight or flight takes hold!

Discussion

Conventional and unconventional thinkers both believe fear is something to be conquered. The difference is in their approach.

Conventional thinkers believe the best way to overcome fear is to face it head on. This is an irrational response. In the jungle, if a lion was about to eat you, it's irrational to face the lion head on to try and overcome it.

Every time fear is faced head on, the fight or flight response is engaged and the mental and physical resolve of the individual becomes overwhelmed by biological response. Overcoming this biological response takes massive effort and energy, and many times conventional thinkers are not up to the task. In the overwhelming overload of their physical responses, their resolve fails, their fear conquers them, and they give up. Over time, repeatedly giving up paralyzes them, and they no longer try to overcome fear. This paralysis, combined with failure, shatters their self-confidence, which further compounds the problem.

Conventional thinkers who manage to overcome fear relish the experience and many attempt to reproduce the physiological fight or flight response by becoming adrenaline junkies to feel the thrill of conquering their fear.

Unconventional thinkers overcome fear by recognizing the important role physiological response of fight or flight plays. Instead of engaging the fight/flight response directly, they first ensure they are calm and relaxed through exercises, such as meditation, hypnosis, or introspective thought.

In these relaxed states, they think rationally and examine what causes them fear and determine what is triggering their perceived danger. When triggers are identified in a calm state of mind, they can change how they think about these triggers without activating the fight or flight response.

The simple act of changing their thinking on what triggers their fear, actually removes the trigger and so they are not forced to go through the physiological response of fight or flight. The fear is conquered without a head-on confrontation, and it's much easier.

In a sales scenario, an irrational response to fear of rejection is the thought that prospects are personally rejecting the salesperson. The rational response is acknowledging that the prospect is not rejecting the salesperson. In reality, the customer is rejecting what is being sold. It's not personal. Because the unconventional thinker recognizes that they are not personally being rejected, the fear and the biological response are not triggered. Thinking about the situation differently, without the head-on confrontation, conquers fear.

Thought Manipulation Action Step for Today

Calm yourself with some deep relaxing breathing for 5 to 10 minutes, and clear your mind. Then calmly think about how you currently approach something that creates fear within you.

Think about the times you've experienced this fear and remember the approach you've taken. Did you confront it head-on? Did you avoid it? Did you spend time thinking about how it dominates you? Did you try to dominate your fears?

Instead of thinking about your fear, think about what triggers your fear and examine these triggers. Decide what outcome(s) you really want instead of the fear outcome these triggers currently produce.

Optional Action Step

If you feel you need help overcoming fear, visit my website at:

http://www.alwaysafraid.com/

There you will find my hypnosis program designed to help resolve fears and phobias.

10
The Law of Emotional Intensity

Definition

When ideas are combined with emotion, the more intense the emotion, the faster the ideas spontaneously tend to realize themselves.

Background Information

When experiencing intense emotion, the conscious gatekeeper is bypassed (see the Law of The Gatekeeper), and the subconscious mind is directly programmed with the ideas and thoughts involved in the intense emotion. The intense emotion itself has a lot of energy, and this energy is transferred into action.

Example

All athletes know that when they become angry a surge of energy overwhelms them, and they perform better physically. Their cognitive abilities may be compromised by their intense angry emotion, but the emotion gives them massive energy to perform. When I swam competitively, my coach purposely used to fire me up to get me angry before a competition. While I was angry, he told me to get in there and beat them. The command programmed my subconscious to beat the competition and the energy of the emotion helped me swim faster.

Discussion

Conventional thinkers believe positive emotions, such as hope, love, faith, and excitement produce success. They believe negative emotions, including anger, fear, shock, stress, sadness and despair, produce failure. The truth is, when they are feeling strong negative emotion, they are focused on failure instead of success. Because their focus is on failure their strong negative emotion brings failure to them quickly.

Conventional thinkers discount the power that negative emotions truly have to motivate and produce results because they have observed negative emotion bringing them failure. They believe these negative emotions should be avoided, and they try to get away from them instead of maintaining the situational awareness required to focus on success while experiencing negative emotion.

Unconventional thinkers do recognize positive emotions are more desirable; however, they know that no one feels positive emotions all the time.

Unconventional thinkers use the power of strong emotions (positive and negative). They harness the energy of powerful emotions and use that energy to motivate themselves and produce results.

When they feel powerful negative emotion, instead of trying to avoid it, they maintain situational awareness and focus on success instead of failure. While focusing on success, the energy of the negative emotion brings them success much faster.

Thought Manipulation Action Step for Today

When you are calm and relaxed, choose an idea of success you want to bring into reality. Summarize this idea in a sentence that you can easily memorize and recite. To program your subconscious mind properly, this should be an idea with language that translates easily into images (described in The Law of Language Translation).

Train yourself to think of this sentence whenever you are experiencing powerful emotions. The more powerful the emotions, the more energy there will be and the faster the idea will begin to realize itself.

Be aware, it's much easier to think of your idea when you are feeling positive because when positive you are already focused on your success. It takes effort to think of your idea when you are feeling negative because you likely feel negative when your focus shifts to something you don't want.

If you recite your memorized sentence when experiencing negative emotion, it is much easier to shift your focus back to success. Then you are free to harness the energy of the negative emotion to produce the successful result you desire. This is not a license to be negative. It's a tool to take advantage of in times when you're stuck in negative emotional states.

11
The Law of Repetition

Definition

An idea must be repeated a minimum number of times before that idea can be effectively programmed into the subconscious mind.

Background Information

The minimum number of times the idea must be repeated (effective frequency) varies. It depends on the person and a combination of this book's multiple laws and cumulative effects. Minimum effective frequency can change simply with a person's desire or aversion to participation. However, the greater the frequency of repetition, the more likely an idea will take hold in the subconscious mind.

Example

Most parents have to repeat themselves many times to get their children to do things they don't want to do. Conversely, when their children want to do something, parents rarely have to repeat themselves.

Think of a time when you had to learn new information. Students studying for exams spend countless hours repeatedly going over the material before they can remember and apply it.

Think of a scenario where you wake up in the morning and as you get out of bed you hit your shin on the bedpost. You say, "I'm having a bad day!" You travel to work and the traffic was congested and you say, "I'm having a bad day!" You realize you missed your first appointment and the customer decided to go to your competitor, and it just cost you money. You say, "I'm having a bad day!"

As the day moves on, you keep repeating, "I'm having a bad day!" It seems like everything you do and say turns into something going wrong. The repetition of that phrase impresses itself on your subconscious, and your day gets worse and worse because your subconscious is responding to your repeated programming and becomes more and more prevalent.

Discussion

Conventional thinkers view themselves as people who find it difficult to learn and change. They find they need to have things repeated numerous times before they get it. The reality is, ideas need to be repeated more because they let their current thoughts, beliefs and habits (all their subconscious programming) interfere with their learning process.

Unconventional thinkers frequently think that they remember things very well and find it easier to learn new ideas and need to repeat things less. This belief stems from their subconscious programming that allows new information in.

Thought Manipulation Action Step for Today

Examine your interaction with people. Do you find you have to repeat yourself or do you find people have to repeat themselves to you to get ideas across?

Think about times that you study and learn new information. Do you find it easy or difficult to remember?

Identify the thoughts and beliefs you have about how well you remember things. Identify how often you have to have things repeated to you.

Remember times where you did not require repetition and remember times where you did. Identify your thoughts and beliefs around both of these times and notice the difference. Begin to focus on ways to use the thoughts and beliefs that are in place when you don't require repetition and apply these thoughts and beliefs to times when you find learning needs repetition.

12
The Law of
Concentrated Attention

Definition

When you concentrate your attention on a thought or idea over and over again, it spontaneously tends to realize itself.

Background Information

Repeated advertising on television, radio, signs, Internet and other places is a prime example of this law. The more the advertising is repeated the more likely you are to buy a product because the more you concentrate on an ad the more dominant it becomes. This programs the subconscious mind with the advertising and then the subconscious responds accordingly.

Repeated advertising can be positive or negative depending on the individual.

Example

Think about buying a car. As you begin to concentrate on buying a car you suddenly start noticing all the car advertising on TV and radio. The more you concentrate on the advertising, the more likely you are to buy a specific vehicle.

Think about seeing food commercials. The more repeated the food commercials are, the more you concentrate on them and the hungrier you get, and the more the visual stimulus makes you want to eat. In an overweight person, the commercials produce desires to eat that can be hard to resist. Conversely, repeated concentration on commercials for weight loss programs can be positive in that it may motivate an overweight person to go on a diet.

Discussion

Conventional thinkers identify detrimental repetitive ideas and attempt to eliminate as many as they can. It's true, the less they concentrate on these external ideas, the less likely these ideas can influence them. But they can't live in a bubble.

Unconventional thinkers identify ideas and determine which ones are positive or negative. They use these ideas (good and bad) to inspire ideas of their own that excite them, and that they can take action on. Fast food commercials entice conventional thinkers to eat. They also inspire the idea in unconventional thinkers that they can eat salads or go for walks instead.

Conventional thinkers let ideas that they perceive to be bad manipulate their actions, and they respond accordingly.

Unconventional thinkers use all ideas and manipulate how they think to create actions that are meaningful and successful for them.

Thought Manipulation Action Step for Today

Pay attention to and identify how many times a day are you bombarded with repeated ideas and suggestions around you.

Ask yourself, how much of what you do and think is actually the result of other people's ideas repeatedly expressed to you? How much of what you do and think actually comes from your own ideas?

Do you perceive the ideas as positive or negative?

Identify all of your own original thinking and ideas that you can repeatedly concentrate on, so you can begin using them spontaneously.

Identify ways you can you take advantage of the ideas around you to inspire new and creative thought to use.

13
The Law of Dominant Belief

Definition

Current beliefs are dominant to new ideas, thoughts and observations that are contrary to those current beliefs.

Background Information

When you believe something completely, it does not matter what the reality of a situation is. The belief will override reality.

It is only when a new thought or idea becomes a belief that it becomes dominant and creates a new reality.

Example

You are walking down the street. Your day was fantastic, and you're feeling great! Suddenly someone mugs you at gunpoint. The mugging happens in 10 to 15 seconds, and the criminal gets away with your stuff. You're physically safe, but your emotions are still charged, making you subconsciously believe you are still being mugged. This belief can last for hours, days, weeks or even turn into patterned thinking where you may never feel safe walking alone again. After the mugging, reality says you're safe, but your subconscious still believes you are in danger and that overrides the reality of your physical safety.

Think about a girl that falls and scrapes her knee. Her mom comes along and sees her girl crying and says, "I'll kiss it better!" When mom kisses the knee, the girl's dominant belief is that mom's kiss will make it better because the child believes her mom. And so the skinned knee stops hurting, and the child feels better, even though the knee is still sore. The belief creates a new reality for the girl.

Discussion

Conventional thinkers who want to make changes in their lives think they should fill their heads with positive dominant thoughts. It makes sense. They've been told that positive thinking is dominant.

Unconventional thinkers believe positive thinking is great, but when they make changes in their life, they know their current beliefs, which they want to change, are dominant over positive thinking. They know it is only when positive thinking becomes a belief that it can create a new reality for them.

Instead of trying to think positive, the unconventional thinker focuses on creating an environment where new thoughts and ideas can become new beliefs. They do this by examining the beliefs they want to change along with the triggers and associations (as described in the Law of Triggers and Law of Association) for those old beliefs.

While conventional thinkers expect positive thinking to do the work for them, the unconventional thinker works to dissociate the triggers and associations with old beliefs that oppose their positive thinking. This work removes the barriers their old beliefs create and allows the opportunity for new thoughts and ideas to become new beliefs.

Thought Manipulation Action Step for Today

Identify beliefs you have that are dominant to new thoughts and ideas in your work, your personal life and your relationships.

Ask yourself, which of your dominant beliefs help you? Which are detrimental? Which dominant beliefs do you want to change?

Address these detrimental beliefs or beliefs you want to change by doing the Thought Manipulation Actions Steps associated with the Law of Triggers and The Law of Association.

Once you have done this work, focus on new thoughts and ideas that you want to turn into beliefs. If you find your old beliefs are still affecting your new thinking, spend more time working on the Law of Triggers and The Law of Association exercises. The more you do this work, the easier it will be for your new thoughts and ideas to take hold and become beliefs themselves.

14
The Law of Reversed Effect

Definition

The harder you try to concentrate on something the less chance you have for success.

Example

Think of a night you had trouble sleeping. The harder you tried to fall asleep, the more you couldn't sleep.

Think about people who want to quit smoking or lose weight. The harder they try, the more they smoke or the more weight they seem to put on.

Think about financial situations. Many people feel the harder they try to make more money and get ahead, the less they seem to have.

Think about sexual dysfunctions, such as impotence. The harder the man tries to perform, the more difficult it is to produce and maintain an erection.

Think about past or current relationships. Remember a time where the harder you tried to make things work, the worse the relationship got. Everything you seemed to do made things worse.

Discussion

Conventional thinkers use will power to overcome reversed effect. Will power is a very powerful tool that has been used to accomplish great things, and it can be effective in overcoming reversed effect in the short term. However, will power requires a great deal of effort, discipline, concentration and sustained energy that most people are not capable of producing long term. If they were capable long term, things like smoking or losing weight would not be rampant in society. There's too much going on in most people's daily lives to continually focus on will power.

Unconventional thinkers use the Law of Association to overcome reversed effect. Past associations incorporate the unconventional thinkers' feelings and ideas to produce different sensory input. This input communicates directly to their subconscious mind and allows their subconscious to respond accordingly and create the effect they want.

For example, when you can't sleep your mind is busy focusing on not being asleep or something else that is stressful. Counting sheep or drinking warm milk works to help you sleep because it produces alternative sensory input that your subconscious had previously associated with sleep. The association frees the subconscious mind to respond and help you fall asleep.

Using established associations (or making new ones if required) guides your subconscious to an alternate desired outcome because that association is the perceived natural course of action.

Smokers using will power to quit smoking still think about smoking constantly. Thinking about smoking generates the reversed effect of wanting to quit. Using associated conditioned response, smokers can associate their currently perceived positive sensory imagery with the positive benefits of being a non-smoker. For example, they can think about enjoying time with their kids or breathing fresh air while hiking in the mountains. The imagery used will be different from person to person because they have individual experiences. Associating positive with positive in the case of reversed effect does not require willpower because it takes advantage of your current beliefs, feelings, associations and ideas.

Thought Manipulation Action Step for Today

Identify a problem you really want to solve but just can't, no matter how much you think about it. Identify what outcome you really want.

Has your thinking become associated with this problem? Identify some positive associations for these problems to guide your subconscious to get the outcome you really want.

15
The Law of Sense Distortion

Definition

Over or under-stimulus of one or more of the five physical senses produces new mental responses — new thoughts, feelings, behaviours and decisions. The over/under stimulus can either be intended or unintended and may last seconds, minutes, hours or a few days.

Background Information

When hypnotizing people during stage shows, I sometimes present a motivational segment of hypnosis for 5-10 minutes at the end to help my volunteers improve their self-confidence. This is a thank you for their entertaining antics during the main part of the show. When I do the motivational portion, many audience members participate because they witnessed the power of hypnosis transforming their friends, coworkers or family members into people who do things they would never normally do.

I begin the motivational portion by using my words to over-stimulate their physical senses. This over-stimulus puts my volunteers and members of the audience who participate in a certain state of mind. They imagine what it is like to have their fears, doubts and obstacles in life removed and replaced with an image of their true self that is confident, positive and at peace with themselves. The overstimulation of their senses puts them in a state of mind where they can consciously and subconsciously react to the positive self-image of themselves. This reaction allows them to produce new mental responses, causing new thoughts, feelings, behaviours and decisions when I wake them up from their hypnotic state.

Many times I've met people after shows or received e-mails or phone calls from people (or their friends) telling me about their new positive behaviours.

I provided a guiding image for self-confidence during the sense distortion for the volunteers. A guiding image is not necessary in sense distortion to stimulate new thoughts, feelings and behaviour, but it is useful if you have a particular goal in mind. A guiding image can be provided by someone else or by the individual experiencing the sense distortion.

Example

Think about the Native American culture. They have mastered sense distortion in sweat lodges and vision quests where extreme prolonged heat and inhalation of smoke from sweet grass or several secluded days in nature can produce focused clarity and visions.

Think about driving a car for a long period. When you get out of the car it still feels like you're driving.

People that have been at sea still feel like they're rocking on a boat once they get on land.

Think about sensory deprivation tanks where floating and the absence of specific senses (usually sound and light) can produce a greater awareness.

Excessive physical activity (the kind athletes do at training camps, not just a five-minute walk down the street) or extreme sports, such as bungee jumping, skydiving and skiing/snowboarding, produce all kinds of sensory distortion.

Try a simple sense distortion exercise where you live. Put on a blindfold, and then move around by feel.

Intimate sexual contact can create sense distortion and so can having a good massage, where relaxation of tension changes the dynamic of a stressed body.

The effects of alcohol and certain drugs certainly can impair or stimulate various senses and create sense distortion.

The list is endless. Pick a sense, and you can find multiple examples to over or under stimulate it.

Discussion

Conventional thinkers usually discover sense distortion accidentally, and depending on the sense distortion, look at it as either a fun or scary experience. They fail to realize they've been presented with a new perception that can ignite their creative process to generate new thoughts and ideas.

If they do realize the potential of sense distortion, they underestimate its value and don't pay attention to the new thoughts, feelings, behaviours and decisions it produces. They may acknowledge and sometimes act on the ideas that seem to pop in their head, but they fail to follow-up and duplicate the sense distortion process.

Unconventional thinkers relish the creation of new thinking and ideas. They recognize sense distortion as a tool that can facilitate this process and actively seek it out. Some are considered thrill seekers, who may bungee jump and sky dive. I do some of my most creative thinking during and after downhill skiing. Thrill seekers' adrenaline rush creates a heightened sense of awareness of self that can open them up to new ways of thinking.

They learn to replicate the process and spend time every few weeks systematically distorting their senses to gain insight and inspiration. There is a fine line where it may become overdone. Becoming physically impaired or sick can happen.

Because the unconventional thinker's goal is to create new thoughts and ideas, they recognize that they can overdo it and take appropriate action to ensure safety.

Conventional thinkers who repeatedly participate are only in it for the adrenaline rush. Many times while pursuing the rush, the conventional thinker ends up hurting him or herself or getting sick. Their focus for sense distortion is different, and so results are different.

Thought Manipulation Action Step for Today

Identify ways you currently create sensory distortion. Identify which ones are intended and unintended.

When sensory distortion occurs, take advantage of it by paying attention to the new feelings, behaviours, decisions and responses you have and take action on the new thinking and ideas you receive.

Which of the sensory distortions you identified are healthy for you and which ones aren't?

When you perform sensory distortion on yourself, how are you reacting to friends, family, coworkers and strangers? Are you reacting positively or negatively? Are you maintaining the relationships you want?

Optional Action Step

Decide on a new healthy sensory distortion method that you can perform to help you generate new and creative ideas and take the opportunity to think differently. Be sure that you remain safe as you do this.

16
The Law of False Memory

Definition

Whenever you repeatedly concentrate on a false thought or idea (your own thought or someone else's), the thought or idea is remembered as true, even though it is false.

Background Information

False memories occur in cases where people have been led by someone to remember something that didn't actually happen. Under interrogation, psychotherapy, hypnotherapy and other situations, false memories can be created with a simple leading question on an emotionally intense subject. The greater the emotional intensity, the more likely the conscious gatekeeper is distracted and the more likely it is to create a false memory.

Example

Think about a time when a police officer needs to get a statement from someone. A general question an officer may ask is, "What did the bad man do to you next." This question can plant a false memory in a person because it has two suggestions embedded into it: "...bad man" and "... do to you next." These suggestions can lead the subject into believing a bad man did something to them instead of naturally allowing the subject to remember.

A question the officer could ask that would naturally allow the subject to remember an event factually would be, "What next?" Even saying, "What happened next?" could make the person believe something occurred just by using the word "happened" coupled with the desire of the subject to please the officer. "What next?" allows the choice of remembering if something occurred or did not occur based on factual memory.

Think of a time you or someone you know had a bad breakup. The relationship failed for bad reasons. But after a period of time, the person focuses on the good things that were present in the relationship. You or they start remembering through "rose-colored glasses" and start creating the false memory that "Things were OK." The two of you may have resumed the relationship because you created the false memory that things were better than they actually were. Then once back in the bad relationship the reality of the bad relationship comes back.

Discussion

Conventional thinkers constantly avoid taking responsibility for their own thoughts and actions. They concentrate on the reasons why things aren't going well. They let their emotions govern their evaluations of facts and make decisions based on how they feel versus logic. Success eludes them and when success comes to other people, conventional thinkers think those people were born lucky, or they cheated, or they come up with any excuse to justify the other person's success. They misguidedly perceive the false reasons why others are successful (like luck, cheating, etc.,) as true and they focus on these false reasons. They fail to evaluate the objective facts of why others are successful. They fail to execute the work involved with real systems of true success. Over time, their concentration on false reasons creates false memory that success is dependent on luck and other non-measurable factors.

Over even longer periods of time, their concentration on untrue reasons for success creates additional false memories. They may think they are successful in some way because they did get lucky or briefly matched some other false reason for success. Once the false memories are created and believed, their ego can't handle the fact that their false luck hasn't brought them the success they desire and crave. They settle.

Unconventional thinkers base their decisions on concrete, proven facts, filtered through their experience and memory. They employ proven systems for success and take responsibility when things go wrong. They learn from their mistakes. They remove their emotions and evaluate mistakes based on objective facts and focus on how to make things better. Their focus on objective fact, in combination with keeping emotions in check, avoids the creation of false memories.

Thought Manipulation Action Step for Today

Think about how you measure success in your personal and professional life. Ask yourself, "How often do I make excuses and focus on why I'm not successful? How often do I take responsibility for my mistakes, learn from them and focus on solutions? In the past when I've made excuses or avoided responsibility, did I create any false memories that influence how I perceive success?"

17
The Law of Visualization

Definition

Whenever you create or see imagery of a thought or idea the imagery helps it improve.

Background Information

Visualization is straightforward. By definition, visualization is creating a repeated mental image of something. Visualization is primarily used to practice a particular activity mentally and improve a physical outcome.

Example

Think about professional athletes. Many of them visualize — golfers, swimmers, football players, basketball players, hockey players and Olympic athletes!

Think about musicians. I've seen piano players use it to practice music without the piano.

Think about self-made entrepreneurs. I've seen many entrepreneurs who use visualization to bolster their self-confidence in achieving tasks.

Anywhere you think you need practice to achieve a specific result, you can practice mentally through visualization and the Law of Language Translation will aid in making more successful visualizations.

If you've never heard of visualization, do a search in Google. There are many millions of resources. Much of the information is anecdotal. But if visualization works for pro athletes, who make millions of dollars, then it can work for you, too.

Discussion

Conventional thinkers rarely rehearse or practice. They spend their time operating on autopilot. They work 9 to 5 doing the bare minimum to get by, collect their paycheck, relax on the weekend and maybe catch a game on Sunday.

Conventional thinkers don't rehearse or practice because they think they're already "good enough." Because they believe they're "good enough," they have no desire or need to improve and the powerful tool of visualization goes under-developed and under-used.

Unconventional thinkers evaluate their own level of skill and competency. Based on their evaluations, they continuously strive to improve. While they usually do have a positive opinion about themselves, they don't view themselves as "good enough." No matter how great they are, they have an inner fire to be better. They constantly work on bettering themselves through practice because they know the more they practice, the better they perform. The better they perform, the better their results. The better their results, the more accomplished and successful they feel. When they're not physically practicing, they do it mentally with visualization.

Visualization is a powerful tool for them. It lets them practice how they want to be successful when they can't physically practice. They set a time (usually at least once a day) where they specifically visualize their success and do it for the pleasure of the experience.

Thought Manipulation Action Step for Today

Pick an activity that you want to be better at. Practice it through visualization for 5 to 15 minutes (or longer if you have the time) one to three times a day for six days. Take the seventh day off. Why take the seventh day off? You rest your physical body. You should rest your mind too. Observe your results when actually doing the activity you mentally rehearse. Note your improvements and adjust your visualizations accordingly. Remember to enjoy the experience. If your visualizing is not pleasurable, then change it. One of the primary goals of visualization is to feel good doing it. That way you get the most benefit.

Do it in a quiet place without distractions, perhaps in a comfortable chair or lying down while wearing comfortable clothing. Reread the Law of Language Translation before you create your visualizations to make sure they produce the image programming you want to communicate to your subconscious mind.

18
The Law of Solitude

Definition

Your visualization to program the mind will likely be more successful if you keep other people or specific events out of the imagery.

Example

Think about a wide receiver playing football. When he is visualizing, he doesn't spend time imagining who is throwing him the ball. If he sees the football only coming from one specific quarterback he would be limiting his mind to catch from only that quarterback. What if his quarterback was injured? What if he changes teams? So he imagines the ball in the air coming towards him, catching the ball and running for the touchdown. He doesn't visualize other players in his path. He imagines a clear path and sees himself running to score the touchdown.

Think about a pro golfer. She doesn't spend time visualizing the competition golfing badly. She imagines herself staying calm, swinging the club and hitting the ball into the hole in as few strokes as possible.

Discussion

Conventional thinkers have a group mentality. They think for a community to thrive they have to imagine themselves as part of the whole and focus on their family and friends as part of their goals and dreams. They dream of success as a group, assuming everyone in their group has the same dream. This disregards the dreams of success of those in the group. They focus on what they believe is right and knowingly or unknowingly force their vision onto others. When their success comes, they don't enjoy it because the other people they wanted to include are not receptive as envisioned.

At this point a conventional thinker will say, "I'm married and have kids. I have to include my spouse and family in my visualizations. I can't visualize success without them." Yes you can! Visualize how good your success feels to you as you enter your house with some of your kid's favourite toys in the background and a present you gave your spouse. This way your subconscious knows your spouse and family are around enjoying the fruits of your success, but your idea of success itself is not forced on them or dependent on their participation to make it happen.

Unconventional thinkers visualize success without being dependent on specific people or events occurring. They view the world as an abundant place where everyone can get what they want. For example, they understand that they love pie, and so they spend their time and effort imagining it, baking it and eating it. But their partner hates pies and loves chili.

Unconventional thinkers respect their partner's individuality. They don't force their partner to bake the pie and eat it. They spend their time making pie and letting their partner make chili. They both eat what they like at the dinner table.

Unconventional thinkers understand that people who want a piece of their success pie will show up to eat, and the ones who don't like it, will eat something else. They realize that including someone who may or may not like pie into their picture of success will limit their picture and make it dependent on someone else. They also realize that when people who do not like pie are forced to eat it against their will, those people will sabotage the pie because they resent being forced to eat it.

Whether on purpose or by accident, unconventional thinkers imagine their goals with themselves as a successful solitary image. They keep their own images and ideas of success for themselves while letting others view success on their own terms.

Thought Manipulation Action Step for Today

Examine one of your visions of success and see the people you've put into the vision. Rework the vision to be solitary so it's dependent only on you and not other people.

19
The Law of Directed Hallucination

Definition

If you excessively visualize a thought that hasn't occurred, you may create a false memory. You'll think it has occurred and make it become a belief that spontaneously realizes itself.

Background Information

A Directed Hallucination occurs when the following 3 elements are combined:

1) Visualization using all five senses to simulate physical reality.
2) High emotional intensity to harness the power of emotions (Law of Emotional Intensity)
3) An altered state of awareness (such as described in The Law of Brain Waves and the Law of Sense Distortion) to bypass the gatekeeper (The Law of the Gatekeeper) to facilitate the creation of new subconscious programming.

When these elements combine, a new dominant belief (Law of Dominant Belief) can be created within your subconscious mind. This dominant belief produces the memory and knowledge that something beneficial actually happened even though it did not (a positive false memory). With the false memory created and believed, the subconscious mind then responds accordingly.

Example

Think about an Olympic athlete. Whether he knows it or not, he creates false memories that improve his sports performance. At elite and professional levels, sports achievement is as much mental performance as physical skill. Creating the belief in the athlete's mind that they can perform at higher levels is just as important as training physically.

To achieve a new level of performance, top athletes must create the belief that they can achieve it. If they don't believe, it can't be done, and they can't make it to the next level. Until 1954, no one believed a runner could break the four-minute mile. Once Roger Bannister broke the four-minute mile, other athletes believed they could also do it. With the belief created, many athletes have been able to take their running to the next level of performance and have since broken the four-minute mile.

To create the belief that the next level of performance is achievable (when believed it cannot be), elite athletes begin with physical practice. Then to prepare their minds, they step up their visualizations to include all five of senses and create intense emotional desires to reach the next level. Their physical practice pushes their bodies to extreme limits, which creates sense distortion. This sense distortion combined with their emotionally intense, five senses visualizations, creates false subconscious memories (a directed hallucination) that the next level has already been achieved. Because their subconscious falsely remembers that the next level has already been achieved, they believe they can do it. Then their subconscious reacts accordingly to this new belief and supports the achievement of the next level of performance.

Directed hallucination really is "visualization on steroids" because it creates new belief where regular visualization only practices and reinforces existing belief.

Discussion

Conventional thinkers create false memories unintentionally to cope with failure. They may have tried using visualization, but their visions don't come true or take a long time because they have not used all five senses and fail to create any emotional excitement. To cope with failure, the conventional thinker may form bad habits, like drinking, smoking or overeating, to feel better. These bad habits are an escape that distracts their gatekeeper and unintentionally allows their thoughts of failure to program their subconscious mind with the false belief that they are failures. These beliefs become mental barriers that keep them from evaluating themselves objectively and they feel worthless and enter a failure spiral.

The unconventional thinker creates false memories to create the belief that greater achievement is possible. This belief produces desire and action that culminates in results that are congruent with their visualizations.

The difference between success and failure comes from the distraction of the gatekeeper combined with visualization that incorporates all five senses and intense emotions equated with the desire to succeed. All five senses and emotional intensity must be included in visualization to mentally simulate what actually happens in the physical world. This simulation creates the perceptual experience of a directed hallucination that is fully realized by the subconscious mind.

The directed hallucination is perceived as real to the subconscious mind and then the subconscious begins reacting as if it were already at the next level. Believing it is at the next level, the subconscious mind then reproduces the physical, mental and emotional environment that it believes it has already experienced.

Even when you have not actually done something, if you remember doing it, then you know it's possible. When you know it's possible, you can take action and duplicate it. Depending on the outcome you desire, false memory in this case is harnessed to serve a constructive purpose.

Thought Manipulation Action Step for Today

Take a current visualization you have (maybe one you made in the Law of Visualization chapter), add your five sensory inputs and emotions to the visualization, and go over it in your mind at least three times. From there, add the positive emotions you equate with that success, including your current desire to achieve this success. The more intense your emotions, the better. To create a new belief in your success, distract the gatekeeper and lower your brainwaves for a new positive false memory in your subconscious mind.

Observe the results and adjust accordingly.

The best order to do the process is right before beginning physical actions:

1) Relaxation to bypass your gatekeeper
2) Visualization
3) Physical action
4) Relaxation and visualization where you mentally correct any lack of physical success you observed during the physical activity.

Be outrageous in your visualizations to help you get to the next level. But do have some objective reality if you want your subconscious mind to accept the new programming. If you weigh 350 pounds and you want to lose 200 pounds, creating directed hallucinations of yourself at 150 could work. But it's very hard for your subconscious to accept that because every time you look in the mirror, dress and weigh yourself your subconscious will be viewing a much different reality. Extreme differences between reality and new programming will negate new programming.

To solve this, go in steps. When you're going up a flight of stairs to the next level, it's always easier taking it one step at a time instead of trying to jump five steps. For example, if you want to lose a large amount of weight, the first step might be visualizing walking for 15 minutes a day and cleaning your cupboards of junk food. Then once you've reached those goals you may visualize eating healthy food and walking 45 minutes a day.

20
The Law of Time Distortion

Definition

Whenever you produce concentrated conscious focus or remove conscious focus, the perception of time changes.

Example

Think of boiling a pot of water. When you have the same amount of water in the same container at room temperature, mathematically it takes the same amount of time boil every time.

When you sit down and watch and wait for the water to boil, your perception of time is distorted. You perceive it to happen slowly and time lags on. However, when you're focused on something else your perception of time is distorted in a different way. Time goes quickly and the water boils in no time.

Think about when you were a student in school or even when you are at work. When you're sitting and watching the clock, waiting for the end of the day, and you want to get out of there, time goes by excruciatingly slowly. But, when you're focused on the work or having a good time, time flies.

Discussion

Conventional thinkers notice when they do what they enjoy, time goes by quickly. They think when doing what they despise time goes by slowly. Because they want to avoid the slow time distortion, they procrastinate and avoid doing things they perceive will go slowly and cause them aggravation and grief. This creates a perception that there never seems to be enough time to do the things they love.

Unconventional thinkers recognize the actual physical passage of time is constant. They know there are only 24 hours in a day, and they make the most of it. They understand to be successful, action must be taken, and they take informed action immediately.

When performing a task, they recognize it is not the enjoyment (or lack thereof) that creates a time distortion. It's actually the amount of focus combined with the amount of action they give to one task versus another task that creates time distortion.

The more action involved in any task, the faster the time distortion becomes. And the less action, the slower the time distortion.

Whether they enjoy or hate a specific task or activity, unconventional thinkers combine their focus with action and do what needs to be done to be successful. They know that if they take action and focus all their attention on the task at hand, time distortion will make the task feel like it goes by quickly. If they produce little to no action, time will go by slowly and they will begin to procrastinate. Where possible, unconventional thinkers will find ways to involve others to help the task occur quickly through help or delegation.

Time distortion creates productivity when focus is combined with action. Time distortion creates procrastination when focus is devoid of action.

Thought Manipulation Action Step for Today

Choose a task you have been procrastinating about. Focus on the task at hand and take immediate informed action. Intensify your focus and increase your action to complete the task as quickly as possible and notice the time distortion. Notice how the time distortion makes you feel when it is completed quickly versus dragging it out and procrastinating.

If the task is large, is there a way you can multiply your action by using a group to perform action with and/or for you?

21
The Law of Distraction

Definition

When persistent stimulus that produces physical, mental, emotional or spiritual pain and stress is present, the pain/stress can be substantially diminished or completely removed by shifting concentration to a new point of focus, even when the stimulus causing pain is still present.

Example

Think about having surgery. Anaesthetic drugs have been developed to reduce or eliminate pain. However, they are not the only option available. During surgery, pain removal in the presence of extreme discomfort occurs through the shifting of focus away from the pain to a new point of focus. The actual point of focus is irrelevant. What is relevant is the intensity of concentration on a new focus that is unrelated to the pain. The intensity of concentration must be great enough that the subject does not revert to focusing on the physical pain. Through the shift in focus, the subject becomes distracted from the pain, and it no longer has any effect on them. If you are not opposed to viewing surgery, a great video that is still available on YouTube is called "Hypnosurgery Live". The URL is:

http://www.youtube.com/watch?v=-s5OFD8uTpU

Or visit my website at **http://www.colinchristopher.com** for the link. It is a 100-minute documentary filmed in England. It goes through the entire process of doctors performing a hernia surgery on a patient using hypnosis as the only form of anaesthesia.

In hospitals in Belgium, as of July 2011, over 8,000 surgeries have been performed using hypnosis for pain control. Go to

http://www.ibtimes.com/pain-and-pleasure-surgical-hypnosis-819023

Or visit my website at **http://www.colinchristopher.com/** for the link.

Many times the surgeries using hypnosis are done in conjunction with anaesthesia. When hypnosis and anaesthesia are combined, fewer drugs are required, patients are conscious, and surgeons report recovery times are faster.

Think about sitting in a dentist's chair. Dentists are beginning to use hypnosis to replace or reduce anaesthetics during drilling and to calm their patients' anxiety.

Many public speakers offer fire walks. The participants train their minds to walk across hot coals in bare feet by focusing on their desires and reaching the end of the hot coals. They are trained over two or three hours to focus on anything but the hot coals so their minds are distracted from the heat, and any pain goes unnoticed.

Discussion

When producing top-level achievement, there is usually an overload of work involved. Professional athletes train for years, sometimes 8-12 hours a day to achieve peak performance levels. Top level CEOs work 60-100 hours a week or more to make their companies successful. This overload of work produces physical, mental, emotional and spiritual stress or pain of some kind.

Conventional thinkers view this pain as something to be avoided and alleviated. When they focus on avoiding and alleviating their pain, they end up working less and feeling more pain because their focus on pain stands in the way and stops them from achieving greater success. They feel they need time off to recuperate, and when they do get back to work, their pain returns.

Unconventional thinkers realize to achieve great success, vast amounts of work are involved and pain in some form will eventually be involved. Instead of focusing on this pain, the unconventional thinkers distract themselves by focusing on the desired end result. This end-result focus diminishes or removes the perception of pain upon work overload.

This makes the unconventional thinker (especially professional athletes) appear to be almost super human in their ability to cope with pain. They seem to be mentally tougher than the average person. They are, and this toughness comes from their self-awareness and ability to relocate their focus from pain to concentration on the end result.

Thought Manipulation Action Step for Today

Develop your ability to withdraw and distract your focus from what is happening around you and focus on the end goal you want to achieve.

Do this by practicing the following:

Perform an activity (15 minutes a day for 6 days) in the presence of mild but manageable irritation or interruption like reading at a noisy park or listening to music you don't like.

The goal is not to read as much as you can, but to shift your focus away from what is interrupting you and instead fully concentrate on what you are doing. Good focus on what you are doing diverts your mind from the interruption.

As you develop this skill, start applying it to situations where you perceive pain or stress by shifting your focus to what you really want to achieve versus focusing on the pain or stress.

The better you become at focusing and concentrating in the presence of interruptions, the easier it will be to distract yourself from and bypass pain. Remember to make sure you're healthy. Pain can be a warning that something is wrong. It's your responsibility to make sure you heed important warnings. You will have to decide for yourself what pain is acceptable to be distracted from and what is something that requires the help of a physician when it comes to your health.

22
The Law of Subliminal Conditioning

Definition

A specific idea can be impressed on the subconscious mind to produce a desired outcome without the direct awareness of the conscious mind.

Background Information

Subliminal conditioning is happening all the time. Your conscious mind can only interpret 40 environmental factors per second while your subconscious responds to 20 million factors per second. Because of this, many things will condition your subconscious without the cognizance of your conscious mind. Examples are: advertising, smells around you, people, how you organize your home and so forth.

Discussion

Conventional thinkers look outside themselves for sources that are attempting to condition them. Whether outside subliminal conditioning is right or wrong, there is a fundamental obstacle conventional thinkers have: they fail to recognize how they are subliminally conditioning themselves.

Unconventional thinkers see subliminal conditioning as a tool to influence their own thinking to achieve their desired outcome. They focus on what they are doing to subliminally condition themselves.

For example, the unconventional thinker who seeks a mate makes sure there is closet space and other space for a mate in a dwelling. Most of the time, they don't think about this space consciously, however their subconscious notices the space that was consciously reserved for a potential mate.   This subconscious awareness subliminally conditions the unconventional thinker to have room in heart and home for a mate. Conventional thinkers seeking a mate keep the space all to themselves, which subliminally conditions their subconscious to have room only for themselves.

In the same way, unconventional thinkers wanting success have reminders of success around them to subliminally condition themselves to be successful. Conventional thinkers look at the success of others and crave it, but do nothing to have any reminders of their own success around them. In the absence of such reminders, their subconscious is subliminally conditioned to the lack of success around them.

Thought Manipulation Action Step for Today

Examine areas of your life where you feel unsuccessful. What reminders of success and lack of success are present? Remove the non-helpful lack reminders and surround yourself with reminders that will serve to build your success.

Reminders of success can be very simple — wearing cologne or perfume that reminds you of success and happiness, placing an award you won out where you can see it or having on your fridge a symbolic picture of your idea of success. Be creative. Your subconscious will notice all these different success stories and respond to the subliminal affirmations of what you want in life.

23
The Law of Framing

Definition

Changing the associated parameters of an idea or situation will change the perception of that idea or situation.

Background Information

Tony Robbins is a master of reframing emotional situations where people are feeling bad or are having other emotional issues. The emotional charge of a situation can be dissipated or eliminated simply by thinking of an idea or situation differently. This changes the frame of reference thereby changing the perception of the emotional situation.

Example

Think about a glass of partially full of water. Depending on your perception, your frame of reference says the glass is either half full or half empty. Empirically (another frame of reference) there is 50% water and 50% air in the glass.

Discussion

Conventional thinkers get stuck in their perception of ideas and situations. They are content with viewing things their way and can't or won't view things differently because they think their current frames of reference are correct. When problems arise, their thinking is limited, and they seek others to help them solve their problems.

Unconventional thinkers are able to examine ideas and situations and discover new ways of looking at things. They realize frames of reference act as points of perception and don't dictate correctness. Changing perceptions stimulates creativity and this creativity makes unconventional thinkers excellent problem solvers.

Thought Manipulation Action Step for Today

Learn or practice your reframing skills by examining current situations that cause you distress. Think of ways you can look at them differently.

For example, if you drive through rush hour traffic and get angry, think of how great it is that you have a car, and you can drive instead of walk to work. The rush hour traffic doesn't change, but your attitude towards it can.

If you're feeling badly about being unsuccessful in a particular area, frame it in a way that you can think about it as a way of learning how to be successful. Thomas Edison made 10,000 non-functional light bulbs before he figured out how to make a working one. You can frame the 10,000 non-functional light bulbs as failures or as learning experiences that, in the end, create a successful outcome.

24
The Law of Least Resistance

Definition

The subconscious mind will take the easiest path to spontaneously realize ideas.

Background Information

Remember, we learned in The Law of Subconscious Habits that the subconscious mind automatically responds to 20 million environmental factors it processes every second in the present. This habitual response becomes the path of least resistance to achieve the realization of ideas.

Think of your subconscious mind as a car. The car's cruise control is your subconscious habits. Every speed you drive at is a different habitual response. One particular idea you want to realize is driving at 80 miles per hour. With cruise control set to 80, your subconscious habitual cruise control responses take over and make sure the car maintains the speed at 80. This allows your conscious mind to drive and focus on avoiding other cars.

Now you come up to a hill. You as the driver are consciously occupied with the environmental stimulus of avoiding other cars and not paying attention to your speed. To maintain your speed, the path of least resistance for your cruise control is to give more gas because that is what it was programmed to automatically do to maintain your speed at 80 while you're busy driving.

Discussion

Conventional thinkers have limited success. During their years growing up they spend the majority of their time responding to environmental indicators of success. This response to environment has formed limiting subconscious habits that say, "Environment determines success." When they attempt to be more successful in the presence of this pre-programmed limit, their subconscious mind takes the path of least resistance and produces results in response to their environment.

When the environment changes and their success falters, the path of least resistance is to seek reasons for failure in the environment instead of seeking reasons for failure within themselves.

Unconventional thinkers examine their achievements. If these results are not consistent with the success they desire, their path of least resistance is to examine themselves and their thinking to see what they are doing. This habit develops through their desire to take responsibility for themselves, regardless of environmental conditions.

While the conventional thinker's path of least resistance is to find fault in their environment, the unconventional thinker's path of least resistance is to take responsibility, change their thinking and create an environment of success.

Thought Manipulation Action Step for Today

Examine your current level of success. Over time, has your level of success changed in response to environmental conditions, or has it changed in response to changes in your thinking?

In areas where your thinking is focused on environmental factors that affect success, find thoughts that allow you to take responsibility for the factors of success in that situation. Then take action on the thoughts that you can take responsibility for.

25
The Law of Perceived Truth

Definition

When an idea is perceived as true, it must realize itself.

Example

Think about racism. It was once believed as truth that white people were better than black people. This perceived truth empowered white people to enslave black people. Slavery stopped when both white and black people perceived the truth that they were equal and fought for that truth of equality.

Discussion

Conventional thinkers view what they perceive as truth to be valid and unchangeable. They accept these perceived truths as reality and don't examine and re-evaluate them. This acceptance of reality makes conventional thinkers slow to change and they become stubborn. In fact, they will fight to maintain their reality, even in the presence of a new truth.

When it comes to success, unconventional thinkers constantly analyze what they perceive as the truth. If their reality is not bringing them success, they examine the validity of their truths. They are quick to embrace new truths when old truths prove to be obsolete, and this responsiveness to change quickly brings them success.

Thought Manipulation Action Step for Today

Examine areas of your life where you are successful. What perceived truths are evident from this success? Examine areas of your life where success is not occurring. Do the perceived truths in these areas coincide with the truths of success you are having in other areas of your life?

Speak to people who are successful in areas where you wish to increase your success, and ask them what they perceive is the truth to their success. Compare these with your truths and decide on changes where appropriate. If someone else's perceived truth brings them success and yours doesn't, their perceived truth must have at least some validity and could be very valuable for you to learn.

26
The Law of Common Sense

Definition

Sound practical judgment applied to new or unexpected forms of environmental stimulus limits thought or action.

Example

When driving, common sense says turn the steering wheel in the direction you want to go, and you'll turn in that direction. When driving on ice and the vehicle loses control, common sense still says turn the steering wheel in the direction you want to go. But when you do this in icy, slippery conditions, you lose control and spin out. To maintain control of the vehicle, you actually have to go against common sense and turn your steering wheel in the direction your vehicle is sliding. This prevents the vehicle from spinning out and allows you to regain control.

Discussion

Great success has many non-predictable factors that are incongruent with common sense. It's a lot like driving on ice.

Conventional thinkers apply common sense in reaction to routine environmental stimulus and get routine results. When non-predictable environmental stimulus occurs, conventional thinkers apply this same common sense expecting it to work. The application of their common sense limits them, and they become frustrated because their common sense tells them they should be more successful.

Unconventional thinkers recognize the validity of common sense. However, they do not apply it when non-predictable factors come into play while pursuing and achieving great success.

For example, it's common sense that an educated person will get a good job and make money. It's also common sense that the more you're educated, the better job you'll get and the more money you'll make.

If this bit of common sense were true, every university professor should be a millionaire. They are some of the most well educated individuals on the planet, yet their incomes do not coincide with the common sense that more education equals greater financial success. Yes, university professors generally make more money than average people because of their education. But no one ever says, "I want to be rich like a university professor!"

In this case, education is certainly valuable, but it's not the determining factor for great financial success.

Common sense says when there is pain, stop doing what is painful; however, the Gold Medal Olympic athlete ignores that, pushes through pain and achieves greatness.

Unconventional thinkers can defy common sense thinking, and this removes the limits that common sense places on conventional thinkers. As a result, unconventional thinkers have one less obstacle between themselves and achieving the great success they desire.

Thought Manipulation Action Step for Today

Examine areas where you feel your success is limited. Ask yourself, are you taking the common sense approach? How is this approach limiting you? What approach can you take that defies common sense?

If you find you are going to extremes, remember to be safe in this. Common sense says, "Don't jump off a cliff because you will die when you hit the ground." If your approach is to jump off a cliff, remember to wear a parachute so you can land safely.

27
The Law of the Comfort Zone

Definition

Current thinking feels comfortable, and this comfort resists changes in thinking when that change is uncomfortable.

Background Information

Changing how you think can sometimes be easy, but many times it's a difficult process because of the effort, time and money involved. This can create discomfort.

Comfort feels good. Because comfort feels good, why would you want to replace those good feelings when changes cause discomfort?

Unless you have some kind of motivation to be uncomfortable, you most likely wouldn't want to cause yourself discomfort.

Discussion

Both conventional and unconventional thinkers have comfort zones. The difference is, when it comes to success, conventional thinkers prefer comfort to effort. They lack motivation/inspiration for change and their preference for comfort keeps them from making an effort to change their thinking.

Unconventional thinkers also want to be comfortable. However, their desire for success motivates/inspires them to choose success over current comfort. They recognize there is going to be a certain amount of discomfort when changing their thinking and actions, but they also realize this discomfort is only temporary. Temporary discomfort is a small price to pay for achieving desired success.

While conventional thinkers let their comfort zones hold them hostage, unconventional thinkers are out there expanding their horizons, challenging their current thinking and actions, and purposely embracing discomfort. They know that this discomfort is a fundamental key to their success.

Thought Manipulation Action Step for Today

It's time to look at your comfort zones. On a scale of poor, fair, good or excellent, how successful are you in stepping out of your comfort zone?

When it comes to success, identify the comfort zones that are keeping you in a safe place.

What comfort zones do you share with your friends and family that keep you thinking and doing the same things?

Do you have sustainable motivation/inspiration to change how you think and act concerning these comfort zones? If the answer is no, it's time look for sustainable motivation/inspiration.

28
The Law of Obsession

Definition

Excessive fixation on a thought makes the thought spontaneously tend to realize itself.

Background Information

Different from the Law of Concentrated Attention, obsession involves an extreme amount of time or focus devoted to ideas or thoughts, to the exclusion of all else.

Obsession that interferes or impairs your ability to work, play, sleep, or your ability to carry out day-to-day activities, is usually considered unhealthy.

Obsession that aids a day-to-day activity is healthy or unhealthy, depending on the observer and extent of focus on that activity. An example is the obsessive desire to check if your stove is off and the lights are out.

Obsession that produces amazing results is usually considered healthy, as found in Olympic athletes, CEOs and others required to perform at high levels.

Discussion

Conventional thinkers seek life balance where they feel the time they spend on their career, finances, family life, friendships, and so forth are in healthy proportion to each other. Balance is great if you want to be mediocre.

Unconventional thinkers are obsessed with their success. Whether Olympic athletes or leaders in successful organizations, they did not achieve great success by being balanced. They spend a disproportionate amount of time eating, breathing and sleeping the success they desire to achieve. They are obsessed with what they do and think, and this obsession aids the achievement of their greatness.

Obsession at this level can create burnout, requiring a recovery period. This recovery period varies and may resemble a period where the unconventional thinker is seeking balance. But once the unconventional thinker has recovered, the obsession calls him or her back to action.

Thought Manipulation Action Step for Today

Are you obsessed with your success or are you trying to be balanced?

If you are trying to be balanced, examine the areas where you desire success and decide if your success in these areas is a true measure of your real desires.

As you examine the areas where you want success answer these questions:

Do you desire to be balanced because you feel stressed and burned out? Are you using balance as an excuse for not achieving success? Do you desire to be balanced because you achieved a great success and you are having a recovery period?

Choose an area of your life where you truly want success and begin to develop a healthy obsession for it, just as athletes and CEOs do.

29
The Law of Physical, Emotional, Mental and Spiritual Pain

Definition

There is a pain threshold. If you pass it — physically, mentally, emotionally, spiritually or a combination of these — you will bypass conscious interpretive response. This allows new ideas to be impressed on the subconscious and/or conscious mind.

Background Information

Everyone has multiple pain thresholds. These pain thresholds are different for everyone and vary depending on stimulus and the different thresholds' interactions with each other. People's thresholds are high, low or somewhere in between. Multiple pain thresholds within an individual vary. For example, a person may be able to tolerate a high amount of physical pain but cry when watching a movie they perceive as painful. Have you ever been on a date at the movies where one of you cried and the other didn't? While two people can watch the same thing, one person can cry while the other can maintain emotional composure because they have different emotional pain thresholds.

When pain is at or below threshold, the conscious mind is active and keeps the subconscious mind protected from unwanted programming. When pain is above this threshold, the pain becomes unbearable and forces the conscious mind to withdraw and protect itself. With the conscious gatekeeper effectively removed, the subconscious mind can be reprogrammed. This programming takes hold and changes in thinking, habits, and behaviour occur very quickly.

An extreme example would be torture during wartime, where prisoners are pushed beyond their capacity to endure pain. To remove this pain, they are forced to renounce their country. The prisoners become brainwashed into doing and saying things they would not do under normal circumstances, and in some cases, they actually believe what the torturer tells them to believe.

Salespeople and late night infomercials employ the "fear of loss" principal to program people to think what they are selling is worthwhile. They offer discounts for a limited time — "Once this is gone it's gone" or "This offer will never be available again." The fear of losing this discount and not ever being able to have what they are offering ever again creates pain in the form of urgency in the individual.

If this urgency surpasses the pain threshold, the conscious interpretive responses of the individual are bypassed and their subconscious is receptive to the words of the sales pitch. The subconscious becomes reprogrammed to believe the product is worthwhile, and this generates the desire to buy, even if the product itself is not worthwhile or useful.

If the urgency does not pass the pain threshold, other types of pain can be introduced to compound the pain until the threshold is surpassed. Many public speakers are good at this. They combine fear of loss pain with other painful emotions by getting their listeners to think about how unsuccessful they are within a particular area (usually in their financial lives). The multiple pains compound each other and push the listener over the pain threshold so their subconscious minds become susceptible.

Discussion

Conventional thinkers do everything they can to avoid pain. Instead of removing the cause of pain by dealing with or resolving the issues that cause them pain, they seek escape.

Seeking escape instead of resolution allows their pains to be triggered in the future when the causes are once again present.

Individual kinds of pain in most cases are not enough to surpass the pain threshold. The issue comes in the presence of multiple pain sources. In the absence of resolving the sources of pain, multiple pains can be triggered. When multiple pains are present they are compounded. This compounding brings the pain of the conventional thinker over their thresholds and leaves them vulnerable. Their conscious interpretive response is bypassed, and this allows them to be reprogrammed with negative self talk or ideas that are not their own.

Unconventional thinkers take an active role in exploring and resolving the sources of their pain. They recognize pain exists and realize the power their pain can have over them. They know not all sources of pain can be resolved, but they don't run away from it or drown it out in creature comforts.

They undergo therapy to remove emotional pain, and if spiritual, they explore their spirituality to feel connected to life and the universe. They remove physical sources of pain where possible, and they pursue mental activities that stimulate their minds.

With sources of pain resolved, they are much less likely to be triggered by multiple pains and do not reach pain thresholds that can result in their subconscious being reprogrammed by inner or outer sources.

Thought Manipulation Action Step for Today

Identify forms of pain (physical, mental, emotional, spiritual) currently occurring in your life.

Make a plan and take appropriate action to resolve as many of these pains as you can. Be reasonable with your actions and plan. While some pain can be resolved quickly, not all pain can be resolved at once. I had chronic physical pain that took me 10 years to fully resolve. But I kept at it, and it did get resolved.

Some things can resolve overnight and others can't. To start, your goal may be to lower the amount of pain you are exposed to or experience so that your pain thresholds are not exceeded. That way you maintain control of what is programmed into your subconscious mind instead of being susceptible to the programming of others.

30
The Law of Pressure Proofing

Definition

In non-critical situations, the conscious, deliberate and repeated practice of particular thoughts or actions in the presence of real pressure, such as stress or pain, increases the ability of an individual to function at peak performance levels when critical situations occur.

Background Information

To achieve great success, pressures like pain and stress will be present. Great success requires sustained peak performance in the presence of these pressures.

Pressure proofing allows an individual to achieve and maintain peak or near peak performance levels whether pressures occur or not.

Example

Think about high level speakers/comedians/entertainers. They rehearse their material so thoroughly that it appears as if they are speaking off the cuff. In reality, every word and intonation is scripted. To add pressure to their practice, they deliver their material in noncritical situations, such as small comedy clubs, Rotary Clubs, Toastmasters clubs, chambers of commerce, or anywhere they can test their material. Once their material is perfected in these non-critical but stressful venues, they become pressure proofed. They are so confident in their material, they deliver it flawlessly.

Think about salespeople. The most successful salespeople work on sales scripts. To pressure proof these scripts and their delivery skills, they role-play with noncritical or simulated buyers to create the stresses of a real selling situation. Once their script and delivery is perfected to the point where it does not seem like they are selling, they become pressure proofed and are ready for real buyers.

Consider airplane pilots. They learn to fly by operating simulators that create unexpected dangers and pressures to allow them to learn to respond without putting themselves in real physical danger. Then, when flying a real plane and real dangers occur, they are pressure proofed and can remain calm to handle the real situation.

Discussion

Conventional thinkers do not realize how important pressure proofing is in the achievement of sustainable peak performance. They know practice is important but do not practice in the presence of the pressures that can occur when peak performance is required.

They recognize pressure can and will occur or be present when they pursue success, but they do not put in the required time, effort and work to be prepared for these stresses. They approach critical situations that are key to their success as a trial by fire and then burn in that fire. Without pressure proofing, they are not prepared to perform at their peak under pressure and achieve great success. This makes their performance suffer or fail completely.

The unconventional thinker has a different approach to critical situations that are essential to success. Before they jump into the fire of these situations, they practice with an intensity that borders on obsession.

Once they feel they have achieved the required level of competence in a particular area, they role-play and practice critical situations. This way they begin to add forms of pressure in small increments allowing them to test their competence. As they role-play/practice they add, little by little, as much real pressure as possible to the simulated critical situations. This increases their ability to withstand pressure and perform at peak levels when real critical situations occur.

Only once they have achieved the appropriate threshold of pressure proofing do they actually put themselves in a critical situation where peak performance is required. They decide when they're ready for critical situations through evaluation and feedback from mentors, coaches and teams of people. They are pressure proofed once they have had enough positive feedback, and they feel they can remain calm, objective, and focused on their desired outcome. Because they are pressure proofed, they appear to do things with ease and grace.

Conventional thinkers do not witness the work, effort, and practice involved in the pressure proofing process. While the conventional thinker is consumed and focused on the stress of failing in their trial by fire, the unconventional thinkers' pressure proofing allows them to remain calm and focused on achieving successful outcomes. By comparison, this alternative focus makes great success seem to appear almost as if by magic. The conventional thinker can evolve their thought process by identifying their desired outcomes and then approaching the situation with calculated objectivity instead of through their stressful emotions.

Thought Manipulation Action Step for Today

In areas where you wish to be successful, identify the factors that create pressure in the performance of thoughts and actions. These factors can include real or perceived physical, mental, emotional, and spiritual pain. For instance, a public speaker having stage fright.

Practice and role-play the activities required to achieve this success during non-critical times. Seek the objective evaluation of trusted mentors, coaches, and teams to provide the guidance you feel you require. Once you are satisfied with your level of competence, sequentially add the forms of pressure you identified while still in a non-critical situation so you can pressure proof your competence. Try adding unexpected forms of pressure to test your pressure proofing. Example: A comedian on stage having the microphone stop working and having to speak loudly so everyone can hear.

Once you are satisfied with your pressure proofing and your competence level, begin performing the activity in critical situations, and notice how much more confident you are and how much better you actually perform.

31
The Law of Vibrational Frequency Attraction

Definition

Different thoughts have different frequencies that reinforce or interfere with each other.

Background Information

From quantum mechanics, we know that every atom generates a specific vibration or frequency pattern. This is based on its negative and positive charges coupled with its spin rate. To modify an atom, you exploit its energy waves by introducing energy of the same frequency. When energy of the same frequency is in sync with the energy of the atom, it creates harmonic resonance causing the atoms to vibrate faster. When energy of the same frequency is out of sync with the energy of the atom, it creates destructive interference that stops the atom. (Lipton, The Biology of Belief, 2005).

Think of what a surfer faces on the ocean. When two waves of water come together in sync near the beach, the resulting wave takes on the energy of both waves and becomes twice as high (harmonic resonance). When two waves of water are completely out of sync and come together, they cancel each other out.

From the law of Brain Wave Frequency, we know that thoughts have individual frequencies. Like an atom in quantum mechanics, to modify the individual thought frequency, you introduce energy of the same frequency (thoughts that vibrate at the same frequency). When these additional thoughts are in sync with the thought you are having, they create harmonic resonance and give each other more energy.

Think of the ocean in the surfer example again: The ocean is your mind thinking. Wave One and Wave Two are similar thoughts that are in sync, and when they come together, their energy combines making the wave twice as high (your thought has boosted energy and so do your results).

When you are thinking about success and your mind decides you can't have that success, your thoughts are out of sync. When you think of a specific result, your thoughts of achievement or failure have the same frequency because they are focused on that same result. But these thoughts of achievement of the result or the failure of the result are out of sync with each other and cause destructive interference.

When a great deal of thought is placed on the achievement of success, the vibrational frequencies combine to create harmonic resonance for achievement of success. Similarly, when a great deal of thought is placed on failure, the vibrational frequencies combine to create harmonic resonance for failure.

When things are going well, they tend to continue going well. When things are going badly, they tend to persist in going badly.

When thinking thoughts of achievement and failure occur at the same time, the thoughts are of the same frequency, they are just disharmonious with each other and create destructive interference where the thoughts cancel each other out.

There must be sufficient thought on the achievement of success to create harmonic resonance. To accomplish this, subconscious habits must be addressed. When the subconscious has been programmed to think of failure, it does not matter how much you consciously think about success because destructive interference occurs. Harmonic resonance occurs when subconscious programming has been changed to agree with and compliment conscious thoughts of achievement and success.

Discussion

The law of vibrational frequency attraction is everywhere, but to conventional thinkers, it's known as the law of attraction. There are a myriad of books describing the law of attraction from The Secret by Rhonda Byrne to The Law of Attraction by Esther Hicks and Jerry Hicks. This law is poorly understood and dismissed by conventional thinkers, primarily because it has been marketed as the easy magic pill that will help you find a parking space in a crowded parking lot.

When the conventional thinker swallows the magic law of attraction pill and doesn't find a parking space every time, right away, they conclude the law of attraction doesn't work.

Unconventional thinkers know and realize the law of vibrational frequency attraction works, but they are perceptive enough to know it's not a magic pill. They know their thoughts can cause harmonic resonance or destructive interference. The unconventional thinker attempts to achieve harmonic resonance in their thoughts, both consciously and subconsciously. They know once harmonic resonance is achieved between the conscious and subconscious mind, belief and physical results occur quickly.

This is why conventional thinkers do not believe that the law of attraction works. They are missing the fact that they have to invest in their thoughts with the appropriate amount of energy and time to achieve harmonic resonance with both their conscious and subconscious minds. The conscious mind is quick to change thoughts, but the subconscious takes time and energy and action to reprogram, as discussed throughout this book. Without making the correct effort, destructive interference always occurs and nothing happens for the conventional thinker.

Thought Manipulation Action Step for Today

Examine areas of your life where you are achieving success and where you are not. Examine your thinking in these areas and ask yourself, "Are my thoughts creating harmonic resonance with each other or causing destructive interference?"

Decide on ways that you can create harmonic resonance with your conscious and subconscious minds and eliminate as much destructive interference within your thoughts as possible.

32
The Law of Colors

Definition

Different colors stimulate different responses and associations to mood, perception, emotion, and decision.

Background Information

The effects and influence of colors on individuals are subjective and based on preference, upbringing, and environmental factors. It is generally observed that the color blue can have a calming effect on people while the color red can excite them. Purple can signify loneliness and desperation while yellow can bring up your spirits. People can be more trusting of a person wearing darker blue combined with yellow. Even though these observations have been made, not everyone responds to these colors the same way. The main constant, however, is that people are influenced by and respond to different colors.

An excellent book on the subject of color is Color Psychology and Color Therapy: A Factual Study of The Influence of Color on Human Life by Faber Birren. The book is out of print, but you can get a copy at Kessinger Publishing's Rare Reprints at

http://www.kessinger.net.

Discussion

Conventional thinkers are influenced by the colors that hold meaning for them and that they like. They seek out and surround themselves with these colors in their homes, work environments, and the clothing they wear.

Unconventional thinkers also do this; however, they also consciously associate success with certain colors (Law of Association). Associating color with their desired success subliminally conditions their subconscious mind (Law of Subliminal Conditioning) to think of success when they see these colors.

Thought Manipulation Action Step for Today

Examine your work and home environments as well as your clothing. Look at the colors that you are constantly surrounded by and ask yourself: "How do these colors affect my mood? What colors can I change to affect my mood to be more successful? What colors do I associate with success? Are these colors associated with success predominantly around me to condition my subconscious mind to be successful? What steps can I take to have more of these colors associated with success around me?"

Change the color of your clothing and notice how people treat and perceive you in these different colors.

Notice colors that people around you wear and decide if those colors affect how you perceive and treat them

33
The Law of Musical Programming

Definition

The melodies and lyrics of music (especially when repeated) program the subconscious mind.

Background Information

We know your subconscious is programmed and responds to the stimulus from your five senses and from the Law of Language Translation. We know language is translated to images and communicated to the subconscious. Music as a stimulus then affects what your subconscious responds to and so do the images lyrics create.

When creating hypnosis programs, music is very important for helping people relax and get into a trance. Once the suggestions for a particular hypnosis program have been heard (usually only 1-3 times is required), the suggestions are then associated with the music in the subconscious mind of the listener. A person can then remove the words of the hypnotist and listen to only the music track, and the music will trigger the subconscious programming that was originally delivered by the words of the hypnotist.

In many cases, just by noticing or reading the lyrics of the music a person regularly listens to, you can predict what a person's subconscious habits will be in the future.

Example

Think about a bad breakup and then think about the music you listened to and identified with. We call the blues the blues for a reason.

Discussion

Conventional thinkers are content to listen to music and lyrics without giving much thought to what is being programmed into their minds by the lyrics. Because they consciously choose the music, they are unaware or dismiss the programming music creates in their subconscious minds.

Unconventional thinkers are very careful about what kinds of programming to which they expose themselves. They regularly find ways to gain new experience and sensory input to expand their minds, and are very selective about what forms that exposure takes. Music is definitely sensory stimulus they appreciate. But they listen to music that inspires them versus music that has lyrics that program their subconscious mind with crude language and negative thoughts.

Thought Manipulation Action Step for Today

Objectively examine the lyrics of the music you listen to. Are the lyrics uplifting, sombre, derogatory, crude, sad, happy or soothing?

After examining these lyrics, look at what is going on in your life. Are there patterns in the lyrics that manifest in your life? If there are, are they contributing to your success or to failure? Or doing nothing?

Decide if you are content with the messages the lyrics program into your subconscious. If you're not, look for music that is right for you, with lyrical content that represents the success you desire. If you find no lyrics that represent the success you desire, listen to instrumental music that feels inspiring to you.

34
The Law of Discipline

Definition

Subconscious habits can be created or overcome with strict adherence to repetition over time.

Example

Think about the military. It has long been true that troubled youth often enter military service to learn discipline to change bad habits.

Think about people who are or were involved in sports. These people are usually successful in other aspects of their life because they learned discipline to do the hard work necessary to excel in the sport.

Think about Thomas Edison. He said his success was a result of 1% inspiration and 99% perspiration.

Discussion

Conventional thinkers believe they are entitled to great success, but they lack the discipline necessary to achieve it.

They think it should be easy to be successful in whatever endeavour they undertake, and if they're not, someone else will help them be successful.

This comes from growing up without learning how to have self-discipline.

In today's society, parents spend more time working and less time raising and teaching their children. They leave the teaching to teachers and expect their children to learn discipline in school.

At school, education standards have been lowered to make things easier for students to pass. Instead of teaching discipline to keep doing hard work until it is done correctly (work done correctly is an excellent measure of success), the educational system in general has made it easier not to do hard work.

The message children receive is discipline isn't important because someone else will make things easier. Being repeatedly exposed to someone else making things easier creates the subconscious habit of entitlement where the conventional thinker habitually expects others to make things easier for him or her.

This entitlement is amplified by commercials that advocate how to make things easier: Fast food commercials, magazine ads that claim vast weight loss in three easy steps in just three days, diet pills that eliminate the need to work out because they burn fat for you, late night infomercials claiming how to get rich in the stock market "fast and easy." Fast and easy is reinforced everywhere, but discipline is not.

For the conventional thinker, this repeated onslaught of fast and easy combined with others making things easy for them, makes discipline the furthest thing from their mind as they attempt to achieve success.

When conventional thinkers do become motivated to do something to make them more successful, the presence of hard work triggers their subconscious habit to take the easy way out because that is the subconscious programming they have received.

Unconventional thinkers who are successful have developed the habit of discipline. It was taught to them in a variety of ways: by their parents, organized sports, the military, a really great school, another organization that requires discipline, or it was self-developed in the presence of an overwhelming desire to accomplish something important to them.

This habit of discipline prepares the unconventional thinker to complete the hard work associated with excellence and success in whatever avenues they desire and choose to be successful. The habit of being disciplined enough to do any and all work necessary to succeed, over time and through repetition, creates new subconscious habits that replace any that are in opposition to success. No matter how strong or daunting any contradictory subconscious habit is, the discipline of the unconventional thinker will prevail, and they will do the hard work necessary.

Thought Manipulation Action Step for Today

On a scale of poor, fair, good or excellent, rate yourself on your level of discipline when completing work necessary to achieve success.

If your rating is less than excellent, hone your discipline by doing a repetitive task or by joining some kind of organized group activity that requires you to develop discipline. Groups are preferred to individual endeavours because you will have the support of and accountability to team members.

As you develop your habit of discipline, apply it to areas of your life where you know long term effort is required to be successful. This will help build the subconscious habits that will aid you to be more successful in those areas.

35
The Law of Will Power

Definition

Whenever you focus sustained mental energy on a specific idea or problem, you generate a specific and desired result.

Example

In a speech at Rice University in 1961, President John F. Kennedy said: "We choose to go to the moon. We choose to go to the moon in this decade and do the other things, not because they are easy, but because they are hard, because that goal will serve to organize and measure the best of our energies and skills, because that challenge is one that we are willing to accept, one we are unwilling to postpone, and one which we intend to win, and the others, too."

It's a great speech and if you want some inspiration, it's available to watch on YouTube at

http://www.youtube.com/watch?v=ouRbkBAOGEw

Kennedy led by instilling inspiration and motivation that generated the "will" to do it.

Will power put men on the moon and is arguably one of man's greatest mental tools for conscious achievement.

Discussion

Conventional thinkers recognize the strength of will power, and they tend to admire it when they see it in other people.

The challenge with will power is it requires continuous conscious effort, especially in the face of obstacles, to maintain focus. As with any skill, maintaining conscious effort and focus takes discipline, practice and at least one of two vital components conventional thinkers lack. They are: 1) Inspiration or 2) Motivation. Without inspiration or motivation there is no sustained will power. There is no fuel to keep the fire burning.

If conventional thinkers were capable of sustained will power, things like smoking and obesity would not be rampant in society and New Year's resolutions would be kept. Conventional thinkers let the activities of their daily lives become obstacles that interrupt their focus and practice of will power. The things they claim they desire don't truly inspire or motivate them. Their desires don't generate the fuel to create sustained will power to produce action and change. Without fuel for the fire, conscious focus is absent and subconscious habits take over. They let their dreams die because they fail to find the fuel for their fire. In fact, most don't even know that they need fuel.

Unconventional thinkers know how to inspire and motivate themselves and others to fuel the fire of will power. But they also recognize that even with the right fuel, their will power is not sustainable in the long run. They know they can't be motivated, inspired, disciplined and practiced enough to have concentrated focus 100% of the time. They need rest, and they take it.

Recognizing this, unconventional thinkers don't hinge their long-term success on will power alone. They do three things:

First, they observe their subconscious habits and determine what happens when their will power waivers. For example, the overweight, emotional eater automatically goes to the fridge or cupboard and eats junk food and repeats this subconscious habit over and over when emotions overcome their will power.

Recognizing these subconscious habits, the unconventional thinker puts a system(s) in place to ensure that when will power wanes, their default behaviour is bypassed. For example, the emotional eater in the presence of will power removes the junk food from their living and working areas, so when will power is gone, there is no junk food to eat.

Second, they create or find a support group setting. The group is designed with the same focus/goals of the unconventional thinker, so there is collective will power. The group helps inspire and motivate each other so that when individual will power waivers, collective-will power can sustain them until they've had time to rest, and they've renewed their resolve. For example, emotional overeaters join local or Internet support groups or exercise support groups that they can call on to help motivate them to get through their momentary lapses of will power.

When you compare collective will power to individual will power, the math of many versus one is easy and unconventional thinkers take advantage of group will power to ensure success.

Third, unconventional thinkers reprogram their subconscious habits so they are no longer obstacles. For example, the emotional overeater seeks a form of action to resolve or reprogram the issues that are associated with and trigger the emotional eating in the first place.

Techniques, such as therapy, are available for reprogramming subconscious habits. Conventional thinkers tend to think therapy is for the weak. Their assumptions about therapy are just more obstacles and excuses that diminish their will power. Unconventional thinkers realize the value of good therapy and use it to their advantage. Of course my preferred technique for reprogramming subconscious habits is hypnotherapy.

Thought Manipulation Action Step for Today

Choose your specific goal or desire for success, one that you believe requires will power which you have not achieved.

Identify if there is enough inspiration or motivation toward this goal to fuel your will power. If not, decide if you really want to achieve success in this area. If you want to achieve, find your motivational or inspirational fuel. If you don't want to achieve success in this area, choose another goal or desire. Be honest with yourself.

Join or create your own group that has the same desires or goals or a group that will at least help keep you on track so you can harness the advantage of collective will power.

Examine your subconscious habits that take over when your will power is not strong enough or absent and use discipline to do what's required when your will power is strong. This will help you ensure success when your will power is waning or absent.

Decide on an action to take that will help you reprogram your subconscious habits. Pick something you feel comfortable with. You should choose an appropriate technique for the habitual behaviours you want to change.

36
The Law of Conscious Responsibility

Definition

Conscious interpretation must be used to monitor and maintain subconscious habits.

Background Information

With environmental stimulus constantly around us, our subconscious and conscious minds process vast amounts of information. As our minds processes this information, the subconscious can reinforce, replace, or make new subconscious habits based on all the conditions it perceives.

Based on these conditions, the physically observable results of success can change and must be monitored and maintained by conscious interpretation

Example

Think of someone who wants to lose weight. They diet, exercise, and eventually achieve their goal weight. It's an amazing accomplishment! But then, with success achieved, they stop paying conscious attention to their weight as they did during their weight loss. Maybe only a little at first, and then a little more, and then next thing they know they've yo-yoed and gained their weight back.

Discussion

Conventional thinkers view success as a destination. They have clear ideas and goals that illustrate what success looks like for them. These are usually based on their observation of how they view other people and the trappings of their success — the big house, the great car, and a lot of money. The person who loses weight gets to their goal weight and thinks all the work is finished. The soon-to-be retiree thinks he has plenty of money.

While these ideas and goals can be indicators of success, once the conventional thinker obtains them, they feel they have reached their destination of success and have no idea what to do next. With no clear path ahead, they let their concentration on their achieved success lapse and stop taking responsibility for their future. After all, they're at the destination. What's left to be responsible for?

The conventional thinker's subconscious has been programmed to reach the destination of success. This programing took place over the long period of time it took to achieve that success. But when they get there and don't know what to do next, the subconscious still perceives that they are trying to achieve the destination because achieving the destination is the default habit programed over time. This, combined with their halt of conscious responsibility for the achieved success destination, allows their subconscious to fulfill its default programmed habit, which is trying to achieve the default destination of success.

In its effort to fulfill this programming, the subconscious mind must create the environment where it can again work to achieve its success destination like it has been programmed to do. The only way to do that is to create an environment where the success destination does not exist. So the conventional thinker with their lapse in responsibility loses that destination of success and asks, "What happened?" The conventional thinker looks for excuses and justifies these excuses by passing the responsibility somewhere else, saying, "How could the economy do this to me and change like that? Fast food restaurants increase the fat content in their food to make it taste better so I eat more and gain weight. That investment banker stole all my money, and I lost everything."

The unconventional thinker views success as a highway that is continuous. To drive the success highway they travel at high speeds and are responsible for themselves. Yes, the unconventional thinker also has ideas and goals that can be viewed as destinations. However, to the unconventional thinker, those destinations are great places to pause and take in the scenery. They enjoy that scenery and then get back on the highway headed to their next destination. Their true measure of success is how well they navigate the success highway to their next destination. They know to navigate that highway means taking responsibility for success. This means monitoring the environmental stimulus around them and how it affects them and the subconscious habits that help them create their success. When their physically observable results regarding success change, they know it's because of something they are doing, saying, or thinking, and they take responsibility for this. Through their conscious interpretation they examine what they are doing, find the problem in their thinking, and resolve that thinking.

Thought Manipulation Action Step for Today

Ask yourself, "With my past successes, did I monitor and maintain that success, or did I stop taking responsibility for myself?"

Make a conscious decision to always be responsible for your success, whether you've already achieved it or are on your way. Make the commitment to yourself to observe whether you create situations that are counter-productive to success. Commit to consciously evaluating your observations, take responsibility, and do the work necessary to be successful consistently.

Most of all, keep the commitments you make to yourself (as described in The Law of Solitude).

37
The Law of Forgiveness

Definition

Healing of past hurts is a powerful way to create new subconscious habits and resolve old ones.

Background Information

Healing your past mental, emotional and spiritual pain requires forgiveness. When there is no forgiveness, the pain endures and the subconscious responds to it accordingly. This pain can be numbed and forgotten by the passage of time, but until the cause of the pain is forgiven, it will eventually be triggered by associated environmental stimulus, and the pain will return. With forgiveness, you'll resolve your pain and no longer trigger it.

Discussion

Conventional thinkers avoid seeking forgiveness and prefer to keep secret what they think requires forgiveness. The reasons for this vary from person to person. They may feel shame, embarrassment, or indignity because they worry what others think. Or they may justify what they've done to the point where they don't think they've done anything requiring forgiveness. They only seek forgiveness when they are caught or when their own feelings of guilt are strong enough to overwhelm. To soften their guilt or to save face, they then apologize and seek forgiveness from others.

Unconventional thinkers only seek forgiveness within themselves. They do not hinge the resolution of their mental, emotional and spiritual pain on the forgiveness or lack of forgiveness of someone else. Because, even though it is possible for an outside source to trigger these pains, the outside source did not create them. Self-forgiveness is the only thing that can heal the pain within and stop the reactions to triggers for the pain. Unconventional thinkers know that when they do not forgive themselves, their subconscious mind will continue to respond with mental, emotional, and spiritual pain. Only once they forgive themselves does this go away.

Make no mistake, apologizing to others they have wronged is important to them, but they realize apologies are only words, and words are not enough. Unconventional thinkers also make amends. They know they can't fix something, but making amends contributes much more to the healing of others and ultimately themselves.

To make amends, unconventional thinkers evaluate the party they have wronged and the extent of the pain they have caused. Based on their evaluations, they do something meaningful for the wronged party or give them something appropriate and valuable.

What determines whether it is appropriate for the situation? Conventional thinkers would say it should be something that makes the wronged party feel better. To the unconventional thinker, appropriate is actually something that makes the unconventional thinker feel better, regardless of how the wronged party feels. What makes the unconventional thinker feel better is grounded in their evaluation of the entire situation. Making the wronged party feel better is usually a result of making amends. But the true goal for unconventional thinkers is to forgive themselves. Feeling better allows self-forgiveness that stops mental, emotional, or spiritual pain, which their subconscious minds have reacted to or with.

Thought Manipulation Action Step for Today

Examine areas of your life where you feel mental, emotional, and/or spiritual pain. If you're not sure where to start, look at areas of your life where you feel guilt.

Identify the external and internal sources of your pain and find ways that you can make amends to others and to yourself in the areas where you want forgiveness.

As you make amends, look at ways you can forgive yourself. In most cases, making amends is enough to help you forgive yourself. If you can't forgive yourself, read the Law of Framing. It gives another way to help you change your view of things and make forgiveness of yourself easier.

38
The Law of Money

Definition

Your perception of money dictates your wealth.

Background Information

Money is the medium of exchange for goods and services, so it is a necessity to live and prosper.

Because you need it to live and prosper, money and wealth are crucial subjects. Almost everyone in developed society devotes a great deal of time thinking about money in one form or another. Whether they have enough, want more, want less, think it's good, think it's bad, money is on people's minds.

The average American family had $3,800 in savings in 2012, according to the federal government. While the U.S. enjoys one of the best qualities of life, people have little savings. It's safe to assume families in other countries face similar circumstances. This means most people around the world feel they don't have enough money.

To get money, most people work and maybe invest some of that $3,800. But that's not much money to leverage.

In summary, you need money. You think about money. Statistically, you don't have enough money, and you have to do something to get money to fulfill the need for it.

The starting point to getting more money and becoming rich begins with your thinking. An excellent book that delves deeply into rich thinking is the best-selling How Rich People Think by Steve Siebold. To really change your thinking about wealth, this book is a must!

You can download five chapters free and get a complete copy at:

http://www.howrichpeoplethinkbook.com

Discussion

Conventional thinkers believe money is something that is received in exchange for their time and effort. They view money as something that has to be worked for. This makes sense. They've gone to school and been told, "To make money, you have to get a good job and work for it." They may be paid by the hour, and they focus on making their money in this one stream of income. If this single stream of income is interrupted because of illness or job loss, they have little or no money.

Unconventional thinkers believe money is something that is received in exchange for many things besides their time and effort. Because they believe money can be made many different ways, they develop many streams of income. Some of the ways they do this are:

1) The exchange of ideas for money. These ideas usually solve other people's problems. For example, people want to be successful. This book is a compilation of ideas to provide tools people can use to be more successful. It was written once and sold many times and continues to sell and make money. There are always problems to be solved. That means there are no limits to ideas for solving these problems and so there are no limits to earning potential.

2) Instead of working for money, they send money to work for them. They invest their money where it makes more money.
3) They leverage the efforts of others. They have many other people trade their time to help them make money. They create businesses that employ people or join network-marketing companies, where the combined efforts of many help them create wealth.

There are many other ways to develop multiple streams of income. Spend some time looking, and you will find them.

Thought Manipulation Action Step for Today

How do you believe you should earn your money? Do you believe you should trade your time for it? Or do you believe you should trade something else to make your money?

You may not be ready to start a business. You may not have money to invest. But you can solve problems with your ideas. Look at people around you. What are their problems? What can you help them solve? Find ways of helping them solve their problems where you can receive compensation. As you do, you will develop the skill of trading your ideas for money instead of trading your time for money.

Develop the belief that your time is yours and look for as many ways to keep your time and create multiple streams of income.

Part III
Social Dynamics
How Your Mind Works
With Others

39
The Law of Ethics

Definition

The morality of thoughts and ideas guide the reactions of subconscious habits and conscious interpretation.

Background Information

In a book about thought manipulation, it seems appropriate to dedicate a chapter to ethics.

In my many years as a hypnotist, there is one question I have been asked by more people (mostly men and some women) than any other: "Can you use hypnosis to have sex with women against their will?" or something very similar.

My answer is, "When I'm camping and light a fire, I can cook food with it, or I can burn down the forest. When I'm on stage, I use hypnosis to entertain, and in seminars or hypnotherapy sessions, I use it to help people. Hypnotizing someone to have sex with me, against their will, is called rape. I don't know how you feel about that, but I use my camping fire to cook, not to burn down the forest around me."

In the introduction for this book I wrote, "Manipulation is the action you take. How you use manipulation to achieve a specific outcome is what's positive or negative."

This book was written with the intention for you to help yourself. Manipulation can be a powerful fire, and can be used in many different ways. It is my hope that you use it to help you cook your supper and not burn down the forest around you.

Example

There are many guidelines to morality and ethics — charters of rights and freedoms, religious documents, tribal and cultural norms, military codes of conduct, children's organizations, the Hippocratic oath of physicians and many more.

Think about it for a minute, and I'm sure you can list at least two or three different influences that currently guide or have guided morality in your life.

Discussion

Both conventional and unconventional thinkers have some kind of self-governing code of morality and ethics.

Conventional thinkers believe their morality is superior. When their morality is challenged, they feel they are right and others are wrong. Their strong feelings motivate them to make others conform to their ethical views. If they cannot convince others to follow their beliefs, they become extreme and attempt to use force on people they disagree with (as described in the Law of Extremes).

Unconventional thinkers concern themselves with doing what they believe is right. What is right for them is what gives them freedom and brings them success. As long as their freedom and success do not interfere with other people's freedom and success, they feel what they think and do is correct.

Thought Manipulation Action Step for Today

Examine your morals and ethics. Are you focused on imposing your morality on others? Or are you focused on letting others do the right thing for them, while allowing yourself to do the right thing for you?

40
The Law of Social Value

Definition

The perceived value of an idea or object becomes greater to an individual or group when another individual or group possesses or believes it is valuable.

Example

Think about children who are playing together with many toys to choose from. The first boy has no desire to play with a specific toy until another boy starts playing with it. Suddenly the toy becomes a must have to the first boy, and he attempts to claim it for himself.

Think about a time when you were in an audience where someone was selling something from the stage. At the end of the sales presentation, speakers use a simple tactic where they say the first five or 10 people will receive a special discount or other amazing incentive. The rush of this first group to buy to get their bargain creates the perception that what is being sold is more valuable. The other people in the audience were unsure of buying or decided not to buy. But when they see people running up, they begin to think it is more valuable and go up and purchase themselves.

Think about the standard view of what is successful in the United States. In general, the perception is that success is having a house, a car, a white picket fence and 2.2 kids because that is what everyone else believes is successful.

Discussion

Conventional thinkers desire ideas and objects that others have. The greater the value others place on an idea or object of success, the greater the value it has to the conventional thinker. Conventional thinkers believe success comes with obtaining what others have, and when they do not possess that idea or object themselves, they become jealous. Once success is achieved, the conventional thinker feels empty and hollow because what he or she thought was the object or idea of success was not really fulfilling.

Unconventional thinkers are unconcerned with social value. They know other peoples' beliefs about success are irrelevant to their own ideas and objects of success. The only opinion that has value to them is their own. They prefer to evaluate ideas and objects of success based on their own desires, and they believe that there is enough for everyone. Their desires are not based on what other people have but on their current needs and whether their idea or object of desire is useful in furthering their bigger picture for success.

Thought Manipulation Action Step for Today

Examine what you believe success to be. Ask yourself, "Is the value of my current ideas or objects of success my own value, or do I find them valuable because someone else has them?"

Determine what you truly desire and pursue that. It makes a lot more sense than pursuing what others have just because you may envy that they have it.

41
The Law of Groups

Definition

When a group dynamic is present, the actions, thoughts, beliefs, and habits of the group become dominant to those of the individual.

Background Information

In the past, our ancestors had a much better chance of survival when they were part of a group than as an individual. Even today, successful modern society is based on mutual cooperation, where we accomplish great things as a group that we could never do individually. As a group, we've gone to the moon, we have complex food delivery systems from farm to grocery store; we have hospitals where we take care of our sick and injured who would not be able to survive on their own. Without the presence of groups, we would be on our own to survive. This translates into an instinctual need for acceptance in order to survive. This instinctual need leads to group conformity.

Example

Think about peer pressure. Kids, adults, co-workers, and even family members will do and say horrible things to lessen peer pressure of a group.

When I perform in hypnosis shows, volunteers are far more likely to perform outrageous tasks when they see other volunteers doing it as well. It's the monkey see, monkey do principle. If other people are doing it, it must be ok, and so they do it too.

Discussion

Conventional thinkers are followers in the group conformity dynamic. They are afraid of voicing their own opinions for fear of rejection by the group. Because of their fear, conformity occurs even when the group's values are contrary to the conventional thinkers' values. Usually, the only time they offer their opinion is when they are asked; and even then, they tend to echo the group's values instead of their own.

Unconventional thinkers are typically the leaders who inspire group conformity. When they are not fulfilling these leadership roles, they are the ones who constantly question and disagree with the group's thoughts, beliefs, habits, and actions. Unconventional thinkers in many cases are catalysts for change, even where their contrary ideas cause them great discomfort, abuse, hardship or even death at the hands conventional thinkers. For example, people like Martin Luther King, Nelson Mandela, and Rosa Parks all championed equality, which conflicted with established thinking of the time.

Thought Manipulation Action Step for Today

Examine the different groups you belong to, such as teams, work colleagues, social clubs — anywhere you socially interact. Observe the thoughts, values, beliefs, habits, and actions of each group. Note the similarities and differences.

Decide which thoughts, values, beliefs, habits, and actions you have taken on from the group, and notice if they are truly your own or if you took them on to conform to the group.

Decide if these thoughts, values, beliefs, habits, and actions are of true value to you in obtaining greater success or if they oppose what you believe is the path to the success you truly desire.

42
The Law of Perceived Value

Definition

There are two values for everything: Actual value and perceived value. Where the actual value and perceived value meet, perceived value is always dominant.

Background Information

The reason a person or group takes a specific action is the value placed on a desired outcome or object is important enough to create that action. In group situations, perceived value for an individual is increased because of the Law of Social Value.

In the comfort of just about all North American homes, there is running water. There is always something to drink and so water has a low perceived value because it is a readily available commodity for a standard price. If you are by yourself in the middle of the desert, the perceived value of one canteen of water is much higher because without that water you will die very quickly.

The amount of perceived value always varies with the perception of supply and demand.

There is an old cliché: "He can sell ice cubes to Eskimos!" Obviously

Eskimos have no use for ice cubes. They are surrounded by ice. However, when a salesperson can create the illusion of perceived value to a customer, the customer will buy regardless of actual value.

Discussion

The conventional thinker's decision process chooses perceived value. Perceived value is influenced by external factors, such as the coaxing of a salesperson and the influence of groups.

The unconventional thinkers' decision process also chooses perceived value; however, perceived value is first tempered through comparison to actual value. This comparison negates external influences, such as social value or salespeople's coaxing, and allows the unconventional thinker to base decisions on their own thinking.

In the absence of comparison between actual and perceived values, the conventional thinker makes decisions based on other peoples' influence instead of their own thinking.

Thought Manipulation Action Step for Today

Think about decisions you've made that apply to anything where the value of something was involved in the decision. For example, these values may be applicable to work, family, education, physical fitness, spiritual guidance, purchases and so forth. Think about the pattern of these decisions over the past three months, six months, one year, and five years.

Decide if these decisions have been made in response to perceived value influenced by other people or if you made your own comparison of perceived values to actual values and based your decisions on your own thinking.

Identify any patterns where you are making decisions on perceived value supplied by others, and begin doing comparisons to actual values. Even if it is too late to change the consequences of old decisions, practicing the process of comparison will give you the ability to do it effectively when external influences exist in the present and future.

43
The Law of Labels

Definition

Predetermined descriptions confine and restrict thoughts and ideas to those descriptions.

Background Information

Labels are everywhere. They have been created to communicate efficiently. However, depending on their intended and perceived contexts, they can be freeing or limiting to an individual.

Example

Think about children. Intelligence labels, where a child is repeatedly told he's stupid can make a child feel labeled as stupid, and they start doing stupid things because they believe that label. When children are told, "You're smart," whether they are or not, if they believe it, it makes them feel good, and it can be very liberating.

Think about people who trip or fall a lot. They say, "I'm clumsy." But are they really? Or are they reinforcing their subconscious belief that they are because others told them that they're clumsy?

Think about people of color. In the Southern United States, up until

1865, this meant they were most likely slaves.   Even in modern times, different colored skin can result in discrimination, racism, and bigotry. Because of terrorism, you only have to go to an airport, and profiling happens based on labels that have been attributed to race and religion. Think about sexual orientation. There are countless labels, which incite extreme reactions, that can be used as derogatory.

Think about political labels such as Republican, Conservative, Democrat, Socialist, Communist, Fascist, and others. These all carry varying degrees of perception and context that can be limiting.

Think about hypochondriacs. Their constant labeling of themselves as sick (combined with The Law of Dominant Belief) can cause the subconscious manifestation of physical illnesses even though there is no real cause of illness. Illnesses are not only limited to physical symptoms. They can have emotional, spiritual, and mental manifestations as well, all because of the perceived label: "You always get sick and catch every cold." As a side note, if you're not a hypochondriac, and you really always get sick and catch every cold, you may want to see a doctor.

One label attributed to a friend of mine is, "Darcy can't remember names very well." He constantly says he's bad with names. Yet when he's paying attention, he can remember the names of individuals he has only met once, in some cases 15 years later. Yet when he thinks he's bad with names he does not think he can remember a person's name he met five minutes before.

Discussion

Conventional thinkers focus too much on labels, especially when interacting with other people. It goes beyond the primary intent of the labels for communication purposes. They use labels to define themselves and other people. When they negatively label themselves and others, negative results show up in their environment. These negative results occur through negative verbal labeling of events that transpire and through negative labelling of themselves or other people.

To the outside observer, the negative verbal labelling of conventional thinkers appears judgemental. They don't spend enough time considering their words or the impact the labels can have. This is because they view their labeling as correct.

The conventional thinker attempts to make others conform to their own labels and views their labeling of things as the way it is. Their internal labels limit them because they believe these limits to be true. Belief in their internal labels causes them to take action and say things that reinforce these labels.

Unconventional thinkers have positive internal labels. These internal labels give them a high sense of self-esteem and inner confidence. This inner confidence translates into others perceiving them as one of a kind and exceptional. Their internal labeling allows them to see past the negative labeling of other people. When new labels come along that can expand their limits, they are quick to adopt the new labels because they recognize labels are only a way to describe something differently.

Thought Manipulation Action Step for Today

Examine ways you have been labelling yourself, other people, and the environment around you.

Analyze these labels and decide if they are positive or negative and if they are really true or if you have been using these labels as an excuse to limit yourself.

44
The Law of the Scapegoat

Definition

Focusing all responsibility on one person or idea for specific outcomes creates weakness within a group.

Background Information

In business organizations, hierarchical structure dictates that managers are accountable for the actions of their employees. In the military, accountability falls to superior officers and commanders. In government, it falls to the leader of the city, province, state, country or other governmental unit.

When things are going well within these organizations focusing responsibility towards the leader(s) and away from the individuals in the group creates dependence. This makes the group vulnerable if the leader is suddenly removed such as in the case of death or other natural attrition within organizations. The resulting power vacuum and lack of direction can create a scapegoat scenario.

When things go wrong within these organizations, blame must be placed somewhere. It's a common practice to shift accountability away from individuals and their actions and make the leader a scapegoat.

Scapegoats are not limited to people. They can also be a description of a larger issue: When things go wrong in the world, common scapegoats are the economy or the government.

Discussion

When it comes to success in group settings, conventional thinkers want to take responsibility for success but not for failure. They hoard information and knowledge thinking one of the secrets to success is not sharing their expertise with others. They mistakenly believe this makes them more valuable. They believe this value will provide them a measure of security within the group.

Combining their need for security and their desire to shirk their responsibility for failure, the group requires leadership that will take responsibility for them. This creates the potential for the scapegoat scenario. When things are going well, this dynamic is not usually an issue. But when things go wrong, the weakness of unshared responsibility surfaces. All faults are shifted to a scapegoat, and the conventional thinkers feel better because they don't have to take responsibility for the part they play or have played within the problem.

Conventional thinkers readily shift their responsibility for things going badly to scapegoats. They expect to be taken care of by their leaders, and they expect things to go well. When things go badly, they feel it can't be their fault, and it must be someone or something else causing the problems. This lack of responsibility leaves the group weaker.

Unconventional thinkers in group settings share responsibility and expertise. They train or teach others within the group so that everyone can be more successful and the entire group can prosper. They believe their security and success relies on sharing because it allows the leaders within the group to concentrate on leadership and appropriate group direction. The more responsibility taken by each individual the stronger the group becomes and the greater their ability to overcome adversity.

When problems occur, unconventional thinkers look at what they are doing that makes them a part of the problem. They look for ways to take responsibility for what they are doing that contributes to problems as a whole. They solve problems from the perspective of what they are personally doing to create and participate in the problems in the first place.

Taking responsibility and sharing makes the unconventional thinker a valuable asset to the leadership of the group and opens them up to promotion.

Thought Manipulation Action Step for Today

In group settings, are you taking responsibility for what you are doing? Are you sharing everything you know that is useful and helpful with the group? Is the group sharing responsibility or is there one person who is responsible for everything?

Identify ways you can share responsibility and knowledge to help the group(s) you are in. Observe the results of sharing your responsibility and your knowledge.

45
The Law of the Victim

Definition

Choosing to believe the control of your fate is a result of circumstances and/or what others have done to you removes your power to act.

Background Information

This should not be confused with extreme circumstances of physical attack or rape for example, where real trauma has occurred. This is in reference to the voluntary assumption of the victim role.

In hypnotherapy, it is extremely common for people to believe the bad things in their life, or the bad habits they have, are a direct result of their unwilling participation in the outcomes that are creating their current life circumstances. They believe they are victims. The benefit of being a victim allows them to draw attention from friends, family and other peers through "Poor me, please have sympathy for my plight" communication. Many times the purpose of assuming the victim role is to create guilt in others, especially family, to illicit sympathy.

Hypnotherapy relaxation techniques allow clients to access their subconscious minds. Once relaxed, they can examine their thought processes and their decisions regarding the situations causing them issues.

Through this examination, they identify the role they played in choosing to become the victim. This allows them to realize how their thoughts and decisions about the issues are making them feel helpless.

This realization allows them to choose different ways of thinking about the situations and issues. This choosing to not be a victim allows the issues to be confronted and the client to take action to remedy their situations. They are no longer unwilling participants in outcomes beyond their control. They become willing contributors to the solutions that will change their lives.

Being a willing contributor shifts emotions to a positive state, away from being the victim, allowing change and healing to occur.

Discussion

Conventional thinkers quickly focus on how other people and circumstances are making them unsuccessful. They believe they played little to no role in their current circumstances, and they are the victims. This places them in a no win scenario, where their prevailing role as the victim (see Law of Dominant Belief) creates further victim scenarios. When success opportunities come, they fail to take action because their victim mentality says something bad is going to happen. If they do take action, something bad invariably does happen because their victim mentality and their subconscious habits make it so.

Unconventional thinkers, regardless of circumstance, identify what role they played that put them where they are. Even when they are true victims and something really tragic happens, they believe it is at least partly their fault for being in the circumstance in the first place. Recognizing their contribution to the circumstance frees them from the weight of negative emotion caused by feeling like a victim. This freedom allows them to remedy what they have done as best they can and move forward by taking action that improves their circumstance.

Thought Manipulation Action Step for Today

Identify areas of your life where you feel like a victim. Ask yourself, "What role have I played in becoming a victim?" and "What benefit has there been for me in being a victim?" Are you able to gain sympathy and attention from others by being a victim? Have you allowed yourself not to attempt things that would make you successful by having the excuse that you are a victim and someone has to help you? Are you waiting to be rescued?

Stop waiting to be rescued and be honest with yourself. Make the conscious decision to get rid of the negative emotions around feeling like a victim by making peace with the role you play and take action that improves your circumstances.

46
The Law of Celebrity

Definition

The credibility and value placed on a person increases proportionally with the fame of the individual.

Example

George Clooney is an excellent example of a celebrity who has used his status to help the world in some way. He has helped fund and increase awareness of a program called the Satellite Sentinel Project. This project was first developed in 2010 as an early warning system to deter mass atrocities by focusing world attention on human rights and human security concerns, mainly in the Sudan. George's celebrity status and belief in the project helped get the project started.

Donald Trump has been very successful, but his celebrity status makes him a household name that increases the value of his business. People buy his books because he is a celebrity. People want to work with him because he is a celebrity. People want to know what he thinks because he is a celebrity. It helps that he is intelligent and successful, but that's not enough. There are many successful and intelligent people, but no one cares what they think. They care what Donald thinks because he's a household name.

Discussion

Conventional thinkers value what celebrities do and think and are influenced by the likes and dislikes of people with celebrity status. Many also crave celebrity status because they believe it is desirable for reasons like ego gratification, lavish lifestyle, sex and so forth.

Unconventional thinkers value their own judgements and perceptions of the success they desire. However, they recognize the power of celebrity status and view it as a tool to help them be more successful. They recognize the potential of this status and leverage the credibility associated with it to make money. Individuals use it to promote their own products (e.g. singers and actors promote fragrances and fashion lines with their own name). Companies use other peoples' celebrity status to endorse their products to create the perception that the product is valuable because the celebrity likes it. Charities use it to help raise funds and awareness with celebrity spokespeople.

Thought Manipulation Action Step for Today

Think about times that you have been influenced by your admiration for a celebrity or wanted to know what a celebrity is doing or thinking.

Decide if this influence is congruent or incongruent with your current desires for success. If you agree with the celebrity, that's great. But if celebrity status is coloring your judgement, refocus yourself and trust that your own judgement is more important than what a celebrity thinks or is paid to promote. Do and think things that make you successful because you want to do them, not because a celebrity endorses it.

47
The Law of Sexual Energy

Definition

We devote vast amounts of energy to the physical, mental, emotional and spiritual drive to procreate.

Background Information

It's no secret that we as a society think about and focus on sex a great deal. It's natural to do so as our very survival as a species hinges on our ability to procreate. It's a biological drive that constantly affects us, and yet views about sex throughout history are polarized. Some believe sexual desires should be restricted, while others believe they should be expressed. There are many books on the topic. We know sex sells, and we know there are many other beliefs and opinions about sex that can be explored. Whatever your beliefs and opinions are, one thing is obvious: A great deal of energy is channelled into sex.

Discussion

Conventional thinkers devote and direct a great deal of their energy towards sex. It is irrelevant whether they view sex as positive or negative. What is relevant is their primary focus regarding sex is on limiting or gratifying their sexual desires or the sexual desires of others. The extent of the limitations or gratifications they express are based on the interrelation of the external beliefs of their family, friends, religion, societal norms, and how these external beliefs resonate or conflict with their own beliefs about sex. Their emotional responses to all these beliefs about sex vary. But whatever their emotional response is it becomes associated with the energy they direct towards sex and associated with their thinking about sex.

Unconventional thinkers devote and direct a great deal of energy towards their success. It's not that unconventional thinkers do not think about or engage in sex, it's that instead of excessively focusing on limiting or gratifying their sexual desires, they spend more of their time focusing their energy on success.

Thought Manipulation Action Step for Today

Ask yourself, "How much time do I spend focused on sex? How much of this time and energy can I direct to creating and producing more success in my life?"

Decide how you are going to manage your time and energy appropriately for you.

48
The Law of the Pick Up Artist

Definition

Friendships, sexual encounters and relationships with desired persons can be created through leverage of perceived value.

Background Information

Many books, websites, social networks, and other media are dedicated to the methodology of pick-up artistry. If you want further information, pick up the books The Game and Rules of the Game, both by Neil Straus. Or check out Neil's website at http://www.stylelife.com/ for much more information about the world of the pickup artist.

Discussion

When it comes to this law particularly, conventional thinkers believe relationships and potential mates are meant to be exploited. They find any means available to seek their own gratification and exploit the people they are able to influence.

Unconventional thinkers use this law to better themselves socially. Unconventional thinking, especially when younger, usually resulted in the unconventional thinker being outside main groups of popularity. Many times they were socially awkward when they were younger and had difficulty with most relationships, especially intimate ones. Using this law they learn how to offer and give of themselves. Their unconventional thinking makes their actual social value very high. However, if they are socially awkward their perceived value to others is low because they are ineffective at communicating their value. To increase their perceived value the unconventional thinker learns these social skills to communicate their true value to others.

The reward of this social learning is the joining of mainstream social groups that the unconventional thinker felt they were unable to meaningfully participate in the past. In some cases this speaks to the instinctual desire to belong to a group as described in the Law of Groups and in some cases it speaks to the desire to better themselves and/or become the leaders in Groups.

Thought Manipulation Action Step for Today

Examine how you interact with people you are romantically interested in as well as your interactions in groups and all other social situations.

On a scale of poor, fair, good or excellent, rate yourself on your ability to communicate well with others in social situations.

If your rating is less than excellent, it's time to develop your social skills so that you can contribute more to the people you know and the social groups you're in. The rewards of contributing will be reciprocated accordingly and your feelings of self-worth and self-confidence will increase.

49
The Law of Spiritual Faith

Definition

When ideas are associated with a higher power, the idea spontaneously tends to realize itself faster.

Background Information

When talking about spiritual faith, I am referring to belief in the divine, not religion. Religion is covered in The Law of Religious Faith in the next chapter. Whether you believe in God, Buddha, the universe, your inner light, etc., spiritual faith inspires thoughts, beliefs, habits and actions that are very powerful.

Spiritual faith is a powerful truth for individuals, and as we talked about in The Law of Perceived Truth, when something is believed to be true, it must realize itself.

Spiritual faith is a trait that originates from within the individual and her belief in an inherent connection with the divine.

Through communication with the divine (usually through prayer - but not limited to prayer), people ask for their desires. In the subconscious mind, a powerful association (see Law of Association) is created where the ideas and desires of the individual combine with the power of truth that spiritual faith represents for them.

This association allows all future thoughts about the divine and spiritual faith to trigger the subconscious mind to begin spontaneously realizing the new ideas and desires being asked for.
Discussion

Conventional thinkers tend to discount the power of spiritual faith. It's not that they believe or disbelieve; it's that they underestimate the power spiritual faith can provide an individual. If they do believe in the divine, their underestimation of the strength of spiritual faith leaves a powerful tool underutilized because they don't see its potential in bringing them success.

Whether they believe in the divine or not, unconventional thinkers recognize the force spiritual faith creates in making success happen more quickly for believers. When they themselves believe in the divine, their belief is unshakable, and they know and trust the divine will provide them with what they ask for. When they don't believe in the divine, they find other ways of bolstering their subconscious to create associations that resonate with their perceived truth to make success come more quickly.

Thought Manipulation Action Step for Today

If you believe in a higher power, are you underestimating the potential of that belief to bring you success? If not, take appropriate action(s) to begin linking your ideas and desires to your spiritual faith to form associations in your subconscious.

If you don't believe in a higher power, what perceived truth(s) are you underestimating that can help success come more quickly? Once you identify them, take appropriate action(s) to begin linking your ideas and desires to your perceived truth(s) to form associations in your subconscious to bring you success.

50
The Law of Religious Faith

Definition

When ideas presented by a group or religious leader are perceived as true and then associated with a higher power, the idea spontaneously tends to realize itself faster.

Background Information

There are many religions with varying belief systems.

Muslims can't drink alcohol, but in Catholicism, drinking wine is a symbol of the blood of Christ and a way to connect with God and Jesus to absolve sin.

In Islam, polygamy is accepted provided all the wives know about each other and the man spends equal time with all of them and treats them equally. In Christianity, only one wife is allowed.

Spiritual faith is a trait that originates from within the individual and the belief in the individuals inherent connection with the divine. Religious faith originates from the individual accepting someone else's interpretation and belief system of how to connect with the divine.

Once the individual accepts a particular religious belief system as truth, ideas and desires appropriate to the adopted belief system begin to realize themselves.

Discussion

Conventional thinkers who readily adopt the religious beliefs of their respective religions find great comfort in being led and told how to achieve connectivity with the divine. Others have paved the way for them, and they have only to follow the path laid before them.

When religious beliefs conflict with beliefs that create success, the success of the conventional thinker becomes limited. This is because religious beliefs are usually dominant to success beliefs (in cases where conflicting beliefs arise). For example, the belief that money and possessions are meant to be given away compared to the belief that money and possessions are part of success are in conflict and this conflict then limits the conventional thinkers success.

Unconventional thinkers who adopt the religious beliefs of their respective religions develop and maintain a broader perspective. They are aware of beliefs that their religion have and of their own developed beliefs about success. They realize the interpretation of the correct way of living by their religious groups/religious leaders may in fact not be true for them. Where there is a conflict in belief, the unconventional thinker makes their own value judgment and decides which belief is more appropriate for their life. This can lead to disregarding some of the beliefs of their religion, or the choice of another religious organization or another spiritual faith that is more consistent with their own developed beliefs.

Thought Manipulation Action Step for Today

Examine your religious beliefs and your beliefs about success. Identify the religious beliefs that conflict with your beliefs about success and decide which beliefs are truly appropriate for you.

If you observe a conflict, decide to take an appropriate action (if it is safe to do so), which may include examining other religions and/or conversion if you deem this to be appropriate.

51
The Law of Authority

Definition

Commands spontaneously realize themselves when they are received from trusted recognized officials.

Background Information

Authority bestows predetermined, socially-given respect to an individual. Authority is usually transferred automatically to people in uniform commensurate with the station in question or to people who have some other way of identifying that they are an authority.

When social respect is transferred, the conscious gatekeeper is bypassed (The Law of the Gatekeeper). This happens because of the expectation put on the person in authority. It is generally believed they have the correct judgement for the authority given to them and that they will act according to the norms of that authority.

In the absence of the conscious gatekeeper, a situation is created where the subconscious mind is receptive to the commands of the individual in authority allowing it to be programmed/reprogrammed.

Example

Think about a lost child. Children are told, when they are lost or something is wrong, to go to a police officer for help because the police officer has the authority and respect to help them.

Think about religious leaders. Priests, reverends, nuns, rabbis and others have a spiritual authority that influences people, and they are expected to behave within a specific code of conduct.

Think about different work environments. Owners, managers, clients, and staff all have different levels of authority, depending on their position within the hierarchy.

Think about an emergency situation. When chaos happens, a powerful tone of voice can allow someone to assume authority and command within the emergency.

On stage as a hypnotist, my primary authority comes from the tone of my voice. This tone, combined with the words I say, is one of the factors that allow me to command my volunteers and begin reprogramming their subconscious minds to participate in my show.

Discussion:

Conventional thinkers in positions of authority have low self-esteem and mistakenly believe the respect for their station is respect for them. Because they crave respect from others, they feel they have something to prove and constantly work to obtain more authority and assert this authority over others. They hold onto and maintain (for as long as possible) any authority given to them because once that authority is gone, the respect that they have received is gone, and they feel empty without it.

There are many reasons for low self-esteem, such as bullying, poor parenting, failed relationships, and others. The solution for the conventional thinker is to gain authority so they can control others and receive the respect their low self-esteem craves.

Unconventional thinkers in positions of authority obtain their positions because they believe they can make a difference with the respect and power that is given to them. They are not attempting to fill a void in their self-esteem, and so there is no compelling desire to assert their authority at every single opportunity. Authority is only asserted when it is necessary because their self-esteem is already high and not dependant on the respect of others.

Thought Manipulation Action Step for Today

On a scale of poor, fair, good, or excellent, rate your self-esteem level.

Based on this rating, look at positions where you hold authority or desire authority. Do you hold/desire these positions to gain the respect of others or because you want to make a difference?

If you rate your self-esteem at less than good, find ways of raising it where you rely on yourself and not the respect of others.

52
The Law of the Politician

Definition

Whether or not an individual is qualified for political office or other prestigious positions, multiple laws of manipulation working in concert will influence the perceptions of a large group and increase the candidate's likelihood of winning.

Background Information

Many public figures running for public office have teams of people who research and gather statistics on what voters think about the candidate and their opponents. Based on this research, the election team creates a plan to change the voter's perceptions of the candidate and their opponents.

The election team will manipulate perceptions through visual associations, voice modulation, celebrity endorsements, musical influence, emotional influence, color perception (clothing and surroundings etc.), and any other tools that can illicit responses from voters. The primary goal of manipulation is to influence voters to like the candidate more and the opponent less. These manipulations make the election process become somewhat of a popularity contest that minimizes real issues and draws attention away from the true qualifications of all the candidates.

To see an example, Google "Obama Superman Picture." You will see multiple results of Obama as Superman or associated with Superman. Superman has been associated to stand for Truth, Justice, and the American Way. These pictures associated Obama with Superman and subliminally communicated that Obama stands for Truth, Justice, and the American Way.

For his first campaign, Obama wore blue ties that were very similar in color shade to Superman's blue tights. Whether done on purpose or by accident, this color also triggered the association with Superman and his standing for Truth, Justice, and the American Way and subliminally equated Obama with Superman.

A much deeper analysis of team strategies used for political candidates can be done, but this is one example.

Discussion

Conventional thinkers vote for candidates based on their feelings about the candidate, the party, and what they believe the candidate and party will do based on promises made during the campaigning process. Because of that, the manipulation process of the election teams more easily influences them.

Unconventional thinkers evaluate the track records of candidates and look for inconsistencies and congruencies in candidate promises and past actions. They avoid the popularity contest election teams create and evaluate the candidates' character to do what they say and say what they do. This discernment allows them to make decisions without involving or minimally involving their emotions about the candidates. This makes it much easier to vote because decisions are based on logical reasoning. Unconventional thinkers have a vision of what they want to see happen in the future and vote for the candidate or party that most credibly supports their vision.

Thought Manipulation Action Step for Today

In past elections, decide if you voted based on your feelings that were influenced by the manipulations of election teams. Or did you vote with logical reasoning about the character, track record, and views of the candidates?

For future elections, pay attention to the laws of manipulation and identify the laws being used by the candidates and their election teams. By identifying the laws they are using, you can eliminate their influence from your decision making process. This way your reason and logic will allow you to select and vote for the candidate who supports your vision and will do the job you want them to do.

53
The Law of Extremes

Definition

When following the middle path, there is balance and prosperity, but when mutual cooperation is circumvented, discord occurs.

Background Information

When examining family life, the workplace, governments and anywhere relationships are present equilibrium and productivity occurs when everyone is travelling the middle path. The middle path offers cooperation and mutual respect, where people focus on creating and doing. When individuals or groups go to extremes, discord occurs because the extremists are focused on what they do not like and what is going wrong. This focus is reinforced in their subconscious, which responds accordingly and gives them more of what they do not like and more of what is going wrong.

Example

Think about religion. It has been said that religion causes wars. But religious organizations and their practitioners do many other things. For instance, they take care of the sick, provide education in places where education is absent, give solace to those in grief, impart guidance for people who want to get married, and provide spiritual direction for those that desire it. So how then does religion cause wars and help people at the same time? It's not the religion. It is the people.

Osama Bin Laden wanted a holy war, but it was not his religion that was the instigator of his crimes. It was his extremism and the extremism of his group that resulted in the terrorist attacks and the events that followed.

When extremism occurs within people it causes discord. The people who state religions cause wars are ignoring and discrediting the good within the religion's people. Making broad negative generalizations about people and their beliefs creates more conflict. This pushes people towards extremism and takes away from their ability to follow a middle path, where the positive aspects of religion can be focused on.

Think about U.S. elections. The polarity between the Republican and Democratic parties and the news coverage of each presidential candidate is extreme. Even on Facebook, Twitter, and other social media sites, the extremes between peoples' opinions turn into name calling rather than focusing on policies and issues that can help them make informed decisions.

Think about successful relationships. In general they are successful because of mutual respect and taking a middle path approach. When one or both members of the relationship are extreme in some way, the relationship tends to have fighting or it ends. Extremes such as ultimatums or blaming problems on the other person create strife. But when the middle path is followed, and responsibility is shared, the relationship becomes better and stronger.

Think about suicide. Suicide is an extreme response to mental, emotional, spiritual and sometimes physical pain. This extreme response is the ultimate discord because its end result does not allow life to continue. When death occurs, the resuming of a middle path, where life can become good again, is not possible.

Discussion

When it's peaceful, conventional thinkers enjoy the drama of extremism.

If they didn't, Charlie Sheen, Howard Stern, Lindsay Lohan and other extreme characters found in tabloids wouldn't be anywhere near as popular as they are. In times of strife, conventional thinkers focus on how they are correct and how others are wrong. They are polarized, see things as black and white, and focus a great deal on what is going wrong and what they do not like. In the presence of this focus, their subconscious gives them more of that. The more they get of what they don't want, the more emotional they become, and the more emotional they are, the more extreme they become.

During times of peace or strife, unconventional thinkers seek a middle path to focus on resolving differences and seeing the shades of gray in between the polar opposites of black and white. They have a broader perspective and look at all sides of issues while examining facts. They evaluate the good and the bad. They focus on solutions to problems and stay away from focusing on extremes. Their balanced approach keeps their emotions in check. This allows them to concentrate on what they want and their subconscious responds to this focus and desire.

Thought Manipulation Action Step for Today

Examine areas of your life where you take extreme views and ask yourself: "Does my extremism allow for the prosperity of others and myself or does it fuel the fires of drama or anger or opposition or hatred? Does my extreme view create charged emotion that keeps me focusing on what I don't want? Or do I remain calm and focus on what I do want?"

Evaluate your views and other peoples' views. Look at the broader perspective to see what you are missing and learn how much you are focusing on what you do not want. Think of ways you can shift your focus to the success you want; success that your extremism is keeping you away from. Find ways to calm your emotions so you can take a balanced approach based on your evaluation of all sides. Take action that allows for your prosperity and success as well as the success of others.

54
The Law of Violence

Definition

The threat of violence minimizes and limits action, while actual violence stimulates intense action.

Background Information

The threat of violence creates fear. In the presence of fear, action is only taken to reduce fear. Because resources are allocated to reducing fear, the real issue (the source of the actual violence) remains unresolved. Once actual violence occurs, The Law of Fight or Flight becomes engaged. By law, the resulting action must be intense to comply with the fight or flight response. In the presence of only fear, fight or flight is not fully engaged, so only limited action will be taken to prevent violence and reduce fear.

Example

Think about a person in an abusive relationship. That person stays in an abusive relationship because they are afraid of what the abuser will do to them if they leave. There is a threat of violence but no actual violence. It's not until the receiver of abuse has enough actual abuse (in some cases actual abuse must be repeated over time) that fight or flight will be fully engaged, and they do something about it. The actual abuse stimulates an intense response, such as abrupt escape and criminal charges against the accused physical abuser. In extreme cases, violence is returned in a severe manner, such as murder (sometimes in self-defence, sometimes in retaliation).

Think about the world before September 11, 2001. Pre 9/11 the population of the U.S. was under threat of terrorist violence within their borders. The country was taking steps to curtail terrorism outside their borders in the rest of the world. But these actions were limited because there was nothing engaging a fight or flight response to the people at home. In general, Americans did not believe terrorism could happen at home.

When terrorist attacks occurred in the U.S. on 9/11, the government and people reacted intensely. Fight or flight response was engaged and intense action was taken through a massive response that involved the invasion of Afghanistan, lengthy war, substantial increase in security at airports and other border entries. An unprecedented allocation of resources was dedicated to the elimination of terrorism.

Discussion

Conventional thinkers focus on the fear that the threat of violence creates. Because of their focus on fear, once violence occurs, they are ill equipped to take rational appropriate response. Their reactions to actual violence are based in fight or flight, and this makes their successive actions intense and sometimes disproportionate when examined from a calm rational perspective.

Unconventional thinkers examine and evaluate threats of violence and look for ways to curtail this violence by providing peaceful solutions to resolve these threats. By creating or making peace with potential causes of violence, there can be no engagement of fight or flight response at a later time because the actual violence will not occur. For example, the court system peacefully tries to resolve disputes. The rule of law is a peaceful solution.

In situations where the creation of peace is not possible, the unconventional thinker creates a plan of action that is based on rational thought before real violence occurs. Should actual violence occur, their fight or flight response can be tempered with a rational plan that has an appropriate response versus an intense action that was or might be, in hindsight, disproportionate.

Thought Manipulation Action Step for Today

Examine the areas of your life where you are threatened with violence. Identify ways that you can safely make peace so that the threat is minimized or eliminated.

Where you can't eliminate the threat, decide on an action plan based on calm rational thinking. Then, should violence occur, you can take a measured response, instead of making an intense reaction.

55
The Law of Transferal

Definition

Qualities and attributes of a person or an object can be transferred to another person through the occupation of the same space or through trusted recommendation.

Example

In NLP (Neuro-Linguistic Programming), it's common to influence others to like you better. To do this, you speak to Person A about person B. You talk about person B's admirable attributes and qualities that you want Person A to perceive in you. While you speak about Person B, you move your hand(s) in front of yourself. Then when you are finished speaking about Person B, you move your body and occupy the same physical space you were moving your hands in. In Person A's subconscious mind, the space where you moved your hands becomes associated with what you were saying about Person B. Then as you move your body into that space, you subconsciously become associated with what you said about Person B (The Law of Association).

As you occupy the same space you were referring to, you take on those same qualities and attributes of person B in person A's subconscious mind. This creates a situation where they like you better and associate you with person B on a subconscious level. Bare in mind, this can also be done to transfer negative qualities.

This is very useful, especially when making first impressions. A major portion of first impressions takes place on a subconscious level. When you meet someone you usually like or dislike them, but you're not sure why. In the blink of an eye, your subconscious mind takes all the information it gathers about the new person and compares it to all the other people you've met. Your subconscious then associates the new person with people from your life that have similar characteristics that you either like or dislike.

When it comes to this law, it's almost as if you are a friend of the person B that is admired. Or you seem very similar to person B, and become familiar in a good way.

It is also possible for your own subconscious mind to take on those attributes and qualities in yourself when you do this repeatedly. Do this just by referring to space near you and walking into it (especially if you do it in front of a mirror so you see it happening to yourself).

Transferral can also take place during a first impression through a referral from a trusted person. Because Person A trusts in the referrer, Person A's subconscious associates that trust with the favourable opinion of you. In Person A's subconscious, you directly take on qualities and attributes the referrer is talking about.

Transferral can also occur when you desire to change your perception in the eyes of people who already know you.

Whether done with someone new or someone you already know, this has to be done carefully. If you overdo it or try to force it people will feel like something is off and will immediately form a negative opinion about you.

Discussion

Conventional thinkers believe that first impressions are dependent on outward appearance, including dressing well, being clean and well groomed, and having a good handshake. To an extent, they are correct. These factors do play a role in first impressions. However, they do only to the extent that they are subconsciously compared to everyone else.

Unconventional thinkers realize that first impressions depend on subconscious comparisons of qualities between them and those admired by the person they are meeting. When possible, unconventional thinkers determine these qualities before meeting a new person. This information can be learned from interviewing common friends or referrers, researching the person on the Internet, or even observing the new person from a distance.

Armed with this knowledge, the unconventional thinker can use the Law of Transferal to influence the subconscious mind of the person they are meeting by transferring the admired qualities they researched to themselves.

One method of transfer is having someone make an introduction. As the introduction is made, the introducer speaks about the unconventional thinker in a positive light, and the new person's subconscious reacts accordingly.

When no introduction is possible, here is another method that works: The unconventional thinker makes small talk about someone that the new person admires. This could be a sports figure, a government official, a friend, or anyone the new person views positively. As the unconventional thinker refers to that admired person, she gestures about that admired person as if they were in front of them.

As the unconventional thinker speaks, she leans closer to the person she's meeting and enters the physical space associated with the admired person. This subconsciously transfers the admired qualities to herself in the subconscious mind of the person she just met.

This stacks the deck in her favour during a first impression or any time she wants to change how she is perceived.

Thought Manipulation Action Step for Today

Think about the last five people you met. Did you like them or dislike them? Identify what you liked and disliked about them and look for these same characteristics in other people you like and dislike and notice the patterns.

Practice talking about people with successful qualities and gesturing to them as if they were right there in front of or beside you while you speak with people. Say one or two sentences about them, and then step into the space where you were gesturing. Observe how the people you are speaking with begin to perceive you. Make it relaxed and casual. If it seems incongruent with regular body gestures or speech, it can create negative feelings towards you.

56
The Law of Reflection

Definition

Your emotional moods will be reflected back to you.

Background Information

It is said that to receive kindness, you must give kindness. To receive love, you must give love. It is true that what you give out emotionally comes back to you. The same goes for all negative emotions, such as hate, anger, and frustration.

The only times emotions are not reflected back are when:

1) The receiver of the emotion remains impartial and maintains self-awareness so their conscious gatekeeper keeps their current emotions intact.
2) The emotion of the giver is so completely contrary to what the receiver is currently experiencing and putting out that it is non sequitur.

Example

Think of a day at work. When a co-worker comes up to you, and you are in a good mood, their mood improves and a good mood is reflected back to you. If you are in a bad mood, your bad mood is reflected back to you.

Think of parents interacting with their children. Children almost always reflect back their parents' mood. When parents are calm, relaxed, and maintain their calmness no matter what their children are doing, their children will stay calm. When parents are aggravated, their children immediately become aggravated and start aggravating their parents more and more.

Discussion

Conventional thinkers tend to take on and reflect the emotions of others. They don't maintain their own emotional integrity and the emotional rollercoaster this creates can be exhausting.

Unconventional thinkers decide their emotional state and maintain it, regardless of the emotions of others. This keeps others reflecting back the emotions they want to see and reinforces their subconscious habits associated with the emotional state they maintain.

Thought Manipulation Action Step for Today

Decide on the emotional state you want and resolve to maintain it no matter the emotional states of others around you.

As you do this, notice how the moods of the other people begin to change and reflect your mood back to you.

57
The Law of Cumulative Contributing Factors

Definition

New ideas realize themselves exponentially faster when the combination of contributing factors reach critical mass. Contributing factors include environmental stimulus, visualization, emotional intensity, beliefs, motivation, inspiration, subconscious habits and others.

Example

Think about Mahatma Gandhi. He believed in his country's independence and believed it could be achieved in a non-violent way. His belief was made exponentially more powerful through the combination of his belief, the power of his emotional intensity, the social and economic situation at the time, and the power of his message.

These factors individually were not powerful enough to reach a revolution, but combined together, they reached a critical mass where the idea of independence in a non-violent way was inevitable.

Discussion

Both conventional and unconventional thinkers achieve critical mass. Unconventional thinkers achieve critical mass faster because they take advantage of cumulative contributing factors to achieve it.

Conventional thinkers believe creating new results is about focusing on the environmental factors that affect them. They work on changing their environment to suit their needs. The time and effort required to change the environment is so substantial that critical mass is unlikely to happen and their ideas and dreams die. If ideas and dreams do finally begin to manifest, conventional thinkers say, "Where has this success been for so long?" The conventional thinker basks in their long awaited success. But since critical mass was so difficult to achieve, with only changing environmental stimulus as the engine for achievement, the energy required for maintaining success wanes and success disappears.

Unconventional thinkers achieve greatness through their attention to the broader perspective. While conventional thinkers are focusing on their environment, unconventional thinkers orchestrate every factor (environmental stimulus, visualization, emotional influence, beliefs, motivation, inspiration, subconscious habits, etc.) they possibly can.

By organizing the individual factors into a cohesive force, they reach critical mass far more quickly than the conventional thinker can. It's like pulling a cart; if you have four horses, the cart is easier to pull than if you have one horse. Through the unconventional thinkers focus and repeated attention to all the factors, cumulative force is created. Because this force reaches critical mass more quickly, unconventional thinkers can begin to duplicate their success in all areas of their lives. It's almost like everything they touch turns to gold. It's not that they're luckier or smarter. It's that they learned to be better at controlling all the cumulative factors to create success more quickly. The more they practice and repeat the process, the faster success comes, almost as if by magic.

Thought Manipulation Action Step for Today

Choose an area where you have been unsuccessful. Determine which contributing factors you focused on to create success and which you have not.

Think of how success in that area will look. Choose at least two contributing factors that you can organize into a cumulative force to reach critical mass and create success in this area more quickly.

Part IV – Case Studies

Please note these case studies have been taken from various places: my performances as a stage hypnotist; hypnotherapy sessions I've conducted, co-participated in, or observed; and from my own personal experiences. These case studies have been included to give you additional real world examples of how the laws of manipulation can interrelate with each other.

The stories have been summarized for the purpose of brevity. In some instances, small details of the case study and/or the sexes of the individuals and all the names have been changed or omitted to protect the privacy of the people involved.

1. Weight Loss

Jeremy was a big man. Six foot four, 380 pounds. In his youth, he was an athlete, and his sport was football. By his late 30s, he was a family man, no longer played football, and had put on 150 pounds since his football days.

Jeremy wanted to lose weight, but he said, "It doesn't matter what diet I do, how much I work out, or what I eat, I just seem to get bigger and bigger."

He was very frustrated and he said, "I feel like I'm too big."

When he was hypnotized his subconscious took him back in time to two important points in his life.

The first was when he was very little and eating supper at the kitchen table. His mother said, "Jeremy, you've got to eat lots of food. If you don't eat, you'll get sick. The more you eat, the bigger and stronger you'll be, just like Dad!"

The second point was when he was playing football in his late teens. His team had just lost a game, and he was talking to his father. His dad said, "If you were bigger you wouldn't get knocked around so much out there."

His parents told him that he needed to be bigger, and whenever he spoke about weight loss, he described himself as too big, and getting bigger and bigger. The Law of Language Translation was communicating to his subconscious that he needed to be bigger, and his subconscious was responding accordingly.

I pointed out Jeremy's language translation pattern, and we changed it to: "I am slimming down while staying strong and healthy." He reported back that he began getting slimmer immediately and within the first month, he lost 15 pounds.

2. Quitting Smoking

Amanda wanted to quit smoking. She had been smoking for 25 years and did not remember why she even started. She tried everything to quit — the patch, gum, quitting cold turkey, and a popular drug on the market.

She knew when she was very stressed she would light up a cigarette. It was obvious there was a direct link between her stress and smoking. In her mind, it was sort of like dominoes. She'd push the stress domino down, and it would knock over the smoking domino. No matter what she did to quit, the stress would always bring her back to having a cigarette.

Under hypnosis and completely relaxed, Amanda spoke as a 14 year old when she started smoking.

She said she was very stressed. Her parents were getting a divorce, and she blamed her mother for driving her dad away. Amanda knew her mom hated smoking, so to get revenge, she started smoking to make her mother angry. Whenever Amanda felt stressed she would smoke.

As an adult, 25 years later, Amanda had an excellent relationship with her mother. However, when her mother was around, Amanda felt more stress and had an overwhelming desire to smoke. When she smoked in front of her mother, her smoking triggered fights. Amanda's job was stressful, too, and that stress also triggered her smoking.

To resolve this issue, I instructed Amanda to visualize a conversation between her at age 39 sitting in the therapy chair, and 14-year-old Amanda. In this visualization, adult Amanda forgave teenage Amanda for her decision to start smoking to make her mother angry.

The Law of Visualization, combined with The Law of Forgiveness, resulted in Amanda's own mind creating the memory that she had forgiven herself.

This in turn resolved her desire to smoke when she felt stressed.
In follow-up she said: "Whenever I feel stressed now, I have no desire to smoke. In fact cigarettes taste disgusting. I haven't had or don't even want a cigarette since the session."

3. Sexual Dysfunction – Impotence

Richard was having a sexual performance issue. In his early 40s, he had been through two divorces and had his fair share of dating breakups. He had been seeing a new woman for a few months but was unable to achieve an erection.

Obviously distressed, he went to the doctor for an examination. The doctor told him there was nothing physically wrong with him and gave him two pieces of paper. On the first paper was a prescription for a sexual performance-enhancing drug you've seen men singing about on television and on the second paper was my name and phone number.

Before filling his prescription, Richard sat down in my chair and told me all about his past relationships. His previous two wives had cheated on him and his self-confidence tanked.

Under hypnosis, Richard revealed the new woman in his life was nothing like the women he had previously been involved with. She was well educated, had a great job, and was an excellent contributor to the relationship. She was a woman that Richard felt was extremely respectable and wholesome, especially in comparison to his former relationships. In fact, in his mind, she was so virtuous that he felt unworthy of her love, and this drove his self-esteem further into the ground.

Richard's inability to achieve an erection stemmed from his thoughts that he was unworthy of his new girlfriend.

Richard was actually a very self-confident man, and he had many things going for him. He already had a strong dominant belief in his self-worth in other areas of his life. In his case, all that was required was a four-sentence script we came up with together that was based on the self-confident experiences of his life.

Under hypnosis, I programmed his subconscious using the Law of Repetition to create a new dominant belief (The Law of Dominant Belief). This new belief was that he was worthy of a relationship with this amazing woman, just as he knew he was worthy of all the other successes that were already in his life.

I never spoke with Richard again, but he did leave me a voicemail message the next day. He said: "It's Richard. Strong like a bull! Thank you."

4. Improving Athletic Performance

I was consulting with a hockey team. These guys were some of the most talented players in the league, but they were on an 11-game losing streak.

I did interviews with the players and the coaches, and it was obvious they wanted to win. No problem there.

I went to game 12 to see how they played. They lost.

After, I went to the locker room, and it was just dead silence. You could hear a pin drop!

I said, "Have you guys ever had trouble sleeping? Did you try everything — counting sheep, warm milk, that kind of thing?

Most of them nodded their heads and said, "Yeah"

I said, "Your problem is what's called The Law of Reversed Effect. It works like this. Think of it with sleep. The harder you try to sleep the more awake you are. It's the same on the ice. The harder you try to win, the more you lose. You're getting the reversed effect."

The guys constantly thought about losing. To manipulate their focus to winning, I had them create the false memory of winning (directed hallucinations). I created scripts for visualizations, based on my interviews with the players and hypnotized them as a group before practice. Their physical practice, combined with the hypnosis and visualizations, were designed to create the directed hallucination of winning in their subconscious minds. After practice, they individually listened to recordings I made for them.

With this false memory of winning (created by the visualizations in conjunction with the sense distortion created during practice) programmed into their subconscious and replacing their losing thinking, they started winning hockey games again.

5. Resolving Fear

Heather was afraid of flying. As a child, she got on planes with ease. However, as an adult she was terrified of flying and would always travel by driving or taking the train.

Her brother was getting married in three days in Hawaii, and she had to be there. She had no choice but to fly.

Under hypnosis, Heather went back to the last time she flew when she was little. The plane was experiencing turbulence. Being small, she actually enjoyed the turbulence and thought it was fun. It reminded her of a carnival ride.

As the plane was experiencing another round of particularly bad turbulence, the man in the seat beside her began to panic and said, "Oh my God, we're going to die!"

Heather saw this man earlier in the flight. He appeared very knowledgeable and intelligent, based on the way he was dressed and carried himself. She felt a great deal of respect for him, admired him, and saw him as an authority figure. She saw him panic and thought if this man is panicking, he must be right, and they were going to die. She began to panic, too.

The turbulence stopped, and the plane landed safely. Heather was freaked out and decided she was afraid of flying. She blocked the memory of the event from her mind and never got on a plane again.   She didn't even know why she was afraid of flying; she just reacted with terror to going on planes.

Heather saw the man as a respectable, authority figure (The Law of Authority). As a result, she viewed his interpretation and opinion of the turbulence as correct, over her own beliefs. She then took on his panic reactions (The Law of Fight or Flight) through transferral (The Law of Transferral) because of her high opinion of him.

To resolve this, I had her relax even more deeply so she felt completely safe. Then I had her visualize a conversation with herself as a young girl on the plane (The Law of Visualization). In the visualization, she asked her younger self to look at how silly it was to give authority to this man and take on his beliefs, which kept her from flying for so many years. It was really his fear and not hers. Her younger self agreed, and together they decided it was time to get rid of that man's transferred terror.

This was done by creating a directed hallucination (The Law of Directed Hallucination) under hypnosis. Heather and the visualization of her younger self got rid of the terror and panic. They did this by putting the terror and panic into a box and sending the box to the sun. As they sent it to burn in the sun, they kept the intention to be calm and happy on any future flights. The directed hallucination programmed her subconscious mind to believe that she could be calm and happy while flying.

Heather felt much better, and three days later enjoyed a relaxing flight to Hawaii for her brother's wedding.

6. Healing the Body

Vanessa had ovarian cancer that was spreading and was scheduled for surgery within two weeks to have her uterus and ovaries removed.

This was a very surprising session because we did very little pre-interviewing. Her goal was to receive healing in whatever form would come.

Under hypnosis, she went back to a young age when she was shopping at the market with her mother. While they were shopping, people in the community were shouting racial slurs at Vanessa and her mother. Vanessa was a mixed race girl, whose father was black and mother was white. This was very unacceptable to society where she grew up.

Vanessa's mother was very protective and strong willed. She argued with some people at the market in front of Vanessa. Vanessa observed that having mixed children was a great hardship for a mother to face. Vanessa decided then never to have children because of the hardship she had seen.

This decision became her dominant belief (The Law of Dominant Belief). To change this, we updated her subconscious mind. We talked about several things: how people currently in her life were accepting of other cultures, that many mixed children have been productive members of society, and how loving and supportive her husband was. By the end of the session, her thinking changed. She now believed it was perfectly all right to have mixed-race children.

Before the hypnotherapy session, Vanessa said her doctor was initially convinced (based on testing) that surgery was the only option left after months and months of ineffective drug therapy.

After the session, Vanessa did not have the surgery and proceeded to have full remission. It is important to note here that Vanessa continued to see her medical doctor and after the session the drugs she was using to fight the cancer seemed to finally begin working.

The only clear thing that had changed was Vanessa's dominant beliefs about having children. It can't be tested at this point, but I personally think it was a combination of her changed beliefs, working together with the drugs that made the difference.

The mental approach to healing is just as important as the physical approach, and I think they can complement each other's effectiveness, as described in the Belgium hospital example in The Law of Distraction.

7. Dealing With Trauma

I was performing at a resort in the Caribbean in a room that was half theatre seating with stage and half nightclub/bar. Ryan was one of my volunteers and was the star of my show that night.

The next morning his wife Sarah found me at the restaurant having breakfast. She said, "Colin, you've got to talk to Ryan. He went through our hotel room last night, broke or smashed everything that had the color red in it, and threw out all my red clothes! My favourite color is red and that's almost everything I brought. I have almost no clothes to wear!"

I asked, "Where is he?"

Sarah pointed to the other end of the restaurant and I started to walk over. Ryan saw me coming and immediately got up and ran away. We repeated this scenario two more times that morning until I was finally able to sneak up on him while he was sitting at a bar at lunchtime.

I sat down beside him before he could leave and gave him the command to sleep and follow my instructions. I guided him to some comfortable chairs, and we sat down. I asked him, "Ryan, why are you throwing out all your wife's clothes and breaking things in your room?"

He replied, "I don't know"

I put him in a deeper trance and under hypnosis he revealed that the red lights on the stage at the show the night before were just like the red lights in a bar he worked at 28 years before. At that bar, he was attacked by a man and got into a knife fight and was almost killed.

For Ryan, the color red was associated with the fight or flight response (The Law of Fight or Flight) he had that night 28 years ago. Now that response was being triggered again by his wife's red clothing and anywhere else he saw the color red.

I hypnotized Ryan even more deeply so that his mind and body were calm and he felt safe. I got him to think about the color red objectively — where he could view the red clothing of his wife as safe, the red lights in the bar at the resort as safe, and the red objects in his room and his surroundings as safe. This allowed him to view the color red in a different way and stopped the triggering of his fight or flight response.

I saw Ryan and Sarah at dinner that night. Sarah was wearing a new red dress Ryan had bought for her that afternoon when they went shopping in town. A few days later, I saw Ryan before he went home. He reported he was sleeping better than he had since that fight in the bar 28 years before.

8. Being the Victim to Control Others

While I was performing, Meghan became so deeply hypnotized that she was too lethargic to be useful in an entertainment capacity during my show. This happens from time to time. The relaxation is just so pleasurable for the volunteer, they want to remain in the relaxed state, and this makes them poor performers for an entertaining stage hypnosis show. I sent her back to her seat in the audience and continued with my show.

After the show Meghan walked up to me with her aunt and her father Ricky, who said, "There's something wrong with Meghan. She seems too relaxed, and she isn't doing what I tell her."

I looked at Meghan, and she seemed perfectly fine. Yet, her father was irate, so I said, "Sometimes people get hypnotized very deeply and need to be put to sleep and woken up one more time somewhere quiet away from a crowd."

We took Meghan to a quiet room without distractions of people, noise and music. Since Meghan was well into her 20s, I asked, "Meghan, do you want to be woken up properly by yourself or with your dad here."

She told me, "By myself."

Ricky got irate and said he would not leave the room. Meghan's aunt finally convinced him to leave.

I quickly put Meghan back into a trance and proceeded with a slower wakeup to allow her senses to adjust. Just as she was near full consciousness, Ricky burst into the room, demanding to know what was happening. As soon as Meghan heard her father's voice, she returned to a deep state of relaxation and did not wake up.

"I'm in the middle of waking Meghan up and you're interrupting the process," I told Ricky. "If you want this to work, you have to leave."

Even angrier, he stormed out of the room. As I started waking Meghan up again, her father burst into the room. Meghan was just about to come to full consciousness, but with his interruption, she fell back into a trance. Strangely, this same scenario happened two more times.

Instead of repeating the process again, I told Ricky to wait in the room with Meghan while I spoke with her aunt outside.

In a 10-minute conversation (with the right questioning), Meghan's aunt told me that Meghan felt her father was always trying to control her and would not let her be her own person. According to her aunt, Meghan gained revenge by finding ways to irritate her father.

It was apparent that Meghan was using her trance state to make it appear to Ricky that something was wrong. She pretended to be a victim (The Law of The Victim) to make Ricky angry and avoid his controlling attitude.

I walked back into the room with Meghan's aunt. Meghan was still in a trance, but we got Ricky to agree to leave again as long as Meghan's aunt stayed in the room. I told Meghan, "I know what you're doing and how you're staying in a trance to make your dad mad. It's time to wake up."

Being caught at her own game of pretending to be a victim, she immediately woke up and was fine.

9. Money and Religious Belief

Roger was an entrepreneur and wanted to be more successful. Every time he came close to a successful breakthrough and was going to make a lot of money something went wrong. He found he was always running out of money, and he wanted to know why.

Under hypnosis, Roger went back to when he was raised in a very poor household with religious parents. His parents were adamant that the best way to get into heaven was to be poor. It was a theme throughout his entire youth until he moved out and began a life of his own. When he moved out, he said he no longer went to church and stopped speaking to his parents. He was so angry with his parents and their religion that he would not even reveal the denomination of faith in which he was raised.

As he examined his potential successes that never happened, a pattern emerged. He realized he felt guilty for having money and would not be worthy of salvation. To alleviate his guilt, he deliberately sabotaged his success to make sure that he did not have money. Subconsciously he still believed what his parents said about poverty being the best way into heaven (The Law of Religion) and his subconscious was responding accordingly.

With this knowledge in hand, Roger was able to observe his actions and thoughts and move forward with a broader perspective that was right for him and allowed him to stop sabotaging his success.

10. Passing the Test and Getting the Job

Rosanne was studying to be an airline pilot. She had grades that put her at the top of the class for written exams, and she knew that she was a skilled pilot in practice sessions. Yet, when she was up in a plane taking practical tests, she would choke and was in real danger of failing.

In practical testing, she said she kept repeating the following words in her head: "Don't be nervous, I'm not going to fail." In fact, she said the instructors used to tell her, "Don't be nervous, you're not going to fail" as they started the tests to try and calm her down.

When she was in regular practice without testing, she said she was able to focus easily on flying because she did not get nervous or feel like she would fail.

Two things were apparent here:

1) During practical exam time, her nervousness was so emotionally intense that the gatekeeper function of her conscious mind was being bypassed allowing her subconscious to be directly programmed.
2) In the absence of the gatekeeper, the phrases, "Don't be nervous" and "I'm not going to fail," were being interpreted by her subconscious (Law of Opposite Language) as, "Be Nervous" and "I'm going to fail."

With this direct negative programming during practical test time, Rosanne's subconscious responded aptly.

All that was required for Rosanne was a vocabulary shift. I hypnotized her and while in a trance she focused on the phrase, "I love flying, I stay calm, and I pass the test."

She went and took her practical flight tests and reported that at the start of the test she felt nervous but kept repeating to herself, "I love flying, I stay calm, and I pass the test." As soon as she said these words, she started calming down, and she did great! She is now an airline pilot.

11. Relationships

Theresa had broken up with the man she thought she was going to marry and was having a terrible time getting over him. It had been two years since their breakup when she found out he was cheating on her. He eventually married the other woman. Theresa was devastated, but she desperately wanted to move on with her life. But she still loved him deeply, even though he was now married and the relationship was over long ago. In fact, she said she felt like she was cheating on him every time she started dating someone new. She wasn't able to move on, and she wanted to know why.

Under hypnosis, she said that when she was out of town for work she felt better, but when she was home, she couldn't stop thinking about him. With more questioning, it became apparent that even though two years had passed, many of the objects in her home were objects they bought together during good times, from artwork on the walls, to the bedding she was sleeping in. In the beginning of the breakup, she had kept the objects in the hope that one day he would return to her, and they would pick up where they left off. This hope was still alive whenever she saw the objects.

Her home surroundings were subliminally conditioning her subconscious that he was still around and that was keeping her from moving on (The Law of Subliminal Conditioning). When she came home from dates with other men, she felt like she was cheating on him, because objects that reminded her of him surrounded her and kept giving her subconscious the subliminal conditioning that he was still there or coming back.

She left the session resolved to remove the artwork from the walls as well as the other objects associated with him and bought new bedding. She immediately began to feel better and think of him less. And within three months, she met another man that she said was amazing.

12. Suicide

I was walking across a bridge in the river valley near my house and came up to a girl. She was maybe 14, crying and covered in blood. She was standing on the edge of the bridge, and I could see that she was getting ready to jump.

I said, "Hi. What's going on? Tell me, why are you crying?"

She said, "I want to jump and kill myself."

I said, "What happened?"

"My brother's dead!" she sobbed. "He died in a car accident. We were in the hospital, and he's dead. He was the only person that cares about me, and now he's dead."

At this point it was obvious that the girl's state of shock and emotional pain had exceeded her pain threshold causing her conscious mind to withdraw and protect itself (The Law of Physical, Emotional, Mental and Spiritual Pain). The primary focus of her language was on killing herself and jumping off the bridge. In the absence of her conscious gatekeeper function, killing herself and jumping was being programmed directly into her subconscious mind and she was ready to jump.

I had to act fast to help her so she would focus on living instead of death. Because of her state of shock and gatekeeper bypass, I knew it was a matter of programming her subconscious with a different picture.

I asked her, "Don't you think your brother wants you to live? Yes?" As I said this, I nodded my head up and down slightly to physically reinforce the suggestion of wanting to live and used the word "don't" (Law of Opposite Language) to further disguise the embedded command of wanting to live.

She said, "Yes." And as she spoke, I nodded "yes" to once again physically reinforce the affirmation of living to her subconscious mind.

While nodding, I said, "Don't you think you will feel better if you live? Yes?"

She started nodding "yes," signalling the suggestion for living was taking hold in her subconscious and coming out in her physical response.

Then I asked, "Do you have any friends or family you can call?"

She did.

I held out my phone and offered, "Come here, you can use my phone and talk to them."

She stepped away from the edge of the bridge, walked towards me, and sat down with me while she called her friend. We waited for almost an hour for her friend to come. While waiting, we talked, and I kept subtlety reinforcing the suggestions of living and feeling better.

Finally her friend ran up. They hugged each other, and cried for her brother.

As they walked away, she turned to me and said, "Thank you"

At no time did I mention certain things to her, such as the words "death," "dying," "jump," or even refer to her being at the edge of the bridge. Remember, she started telling me what was wrong when I said, "Tell me why you are crying." She walked over to me when I said, "Come here. You can use my phone and talk to them." I avoided saying, "Step away from the edge" because it would have drawn attention to jumping instead of keeping her attention on coming to me where it was safe.

At no point did I move towards her. I was calm, spoke in relaxed tones, and let her make her own move towards me. At the same time, I kept her subconscious focused on living and on calling her friend. Coming to me to call her friend moved her away from the edge and distracted her from her emotional pain (The Law of Distraction) and her desire to jump only moments before.

It was a matter of staying calm and focused on the end result and not on the current circumstances (The Law of Pressure Proofing).

Afterword

There is a great deal of information here. You may or may not agree with it. It is my sincerest hope that you take what you have read and use it to discover how you have been reacting to your environment and to your own thinking. When you are reacting without conscious awareness, you are being manipulated by your current subconscious programming.

Again, manipulation itself is not positive or negative; it is the outcome of manipulation that is most important. Take what is here and use it to become consciously aware of how you are reacting. As your conscious awareness increases, you will be able to change your thinking and manipulate your subconscious to react the way you desire.

Again, I wish you great success!

Thank you for reading my book.

Colin Christopher
Edmonton, Alberta, Canada
December 12, 2012

Learning Resources

Free Weight Loss Program Using Hypnosis:
http://www.freeloseweighthypnosis.com/

Always Afraid? Conquer Your Fear Using Hypnosis:
http://www.alwaysafraid.com/

Free Hypnotist Course:
http://www.freehypnotistcourse.com/

Hypnosis Health Store:
http://www.hypnosishealthstore.com/

Colin Christopher's Official Hypnosis Site:
http://www.colinchristopher.com/

Colin Christopher's Success Through Manipulation Speaking Site:
http://www.successthroughmanipulation.com/

Success Through Manipulation Blog:
http://www.successthroughmanipulationblog.com/

Facebook:
http://www.facebook.com/colinchristopher/

Twitter:
http://www.twitter.com/colinontv/

LinkedIn:
http://www.linkedin.com/in/colinchristopher/

LOSE WEIGHT WITH HYPNOSIS FOR FREE

In the news today, they say obesity is an epidemic. If this is true for you and you want to lose weight, there is help. And it's FREE.

When it comes to weight, lighter people think differently than heavier people. Because they think differently, lighter people don't have the mental barriers that heavier people do.

Using this FREE hypnosis program, you're going to put your mind and body into a relaxed state. Then you're going to train your subconscious mind to think like lighter people do. That way you can break through the mental barriers that are keeping you heavy!

www.freeloseweighthypnosis.com

ALWAYS AFRAID?
CONQUER YOUR FEAR!

Does Fear hold you back? Do you have anxiety?
Phobia's get you down?

Stage Fright?   Bees?
Snakes?   Anxiety?
Spiders?   Phobia?

What are you afraid of?

There is help. You're not alone.

Ever wonder why you're afraid of something and someone else isn't? It's
because they react differently than you do. Change how you react so you are
comfortable and calm.

Using this hypnosis program, you're going to put your mind and body
into a relaxed state to train your subconscious mind and change your
fight or flight response. That way you can break through the mental
barriers that make you afraid!

Try it. It's safe. It's relaxing. You have nothing to fear but fear itself!

www.alwaysafraid.com

LEARN HOW TO BECOME A STAGE HYPNOTIST FOR FREE!

Love hypnosis or just curious how it works?

Colin Christopher has been in front of over 250,000 people all over the world and has performed for cruise lines, resorts, casinos, corporations, and more. He is a stage hypnosis instructor certified by The American Council of Hypnotist Examiners and a practicing clinical hypnotherapist who will show you what it takes to be a successful hypnotist.

In this FREE online course you will learn:

What it takes to get started in the business
How to run successful shows and seminars from start to finish
What hypnosis is and how it works
Why you should learn hypnotherapy
What can go right and what can go wrong in your shows
How to write successful hypnosis scripts
The ins and outs of creating self help products
How to market yourself to cruise ships, resorts, casinos, corporations, or any other client you want

…and much, much more!

Sign up today! It's FREE.

www.freehypnotistcourse.com

HYPNOSIS HEALTH STORE

GET YOUR HEAD IN THE GAME AND HELP YOURSELF GET HEALTHY WITH HYPNOSIS!

Quit Smoking • Lose Weight • Become a Better Athlete • Improve Self Confidence • Study Better • Reduce Stress

And more…

Based on his experience as a clinical hypnotherapist and stage hypnotist, Colin Christopher has developed many excellent hypnosis self help programs

These programs work by putting your mind and body into a relaxed state. Once you're relaxed, Colin's hypnosis suggestions train your subconscious mind to think differently and focus your thinking to razor sharp clarity.

When you change how you think your mental barriers disappear!

Try before you buy. It's FREE to download Colin's hypnosis relaxation program. To get your free hypnosis relaxation program, visit the site and enter your name and e-mail address. The program will be e-mailed right to your inbox for FREE.

See how you like it. If you like the relaxation, you'll LOVE Colin's other self-help programs!

www.hypnosishealthstore.com

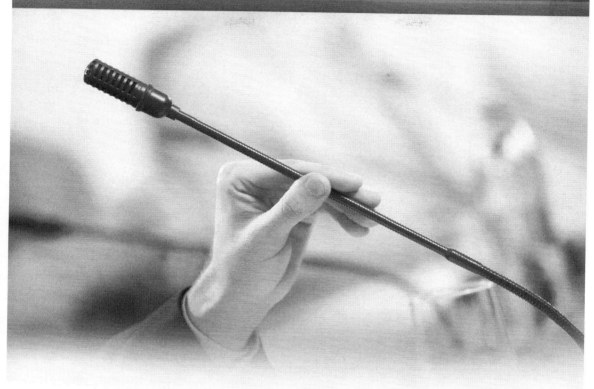

SUCCESS through MANIPULATION
It's not what you think it is. It's about HOW YOU THINK.

FREE VIDEO UPDATES

about
SUCCESS through MANIPULATION
with Colin Christopher

SUBSCRIBE TODAY FOR FREE!

www.successthroughmanipulationblog.com

GET SOCIAL AND STAY INFORMED

Facebook:

www.facebook.com/colinchristopher/

Twitter:

www.twitter.com/colinontv/

LinkedIn:

www.linkedin.com/in/colinchristopher/

About the Author

Colin Christopher has been in front of over 250,000 people throughout North America. Over the last 14 years he has shared stages with world-class speakers like Bob Proctor, Steve Siebold and Brian Tracy. Some of his clients include McDonalds, Bell Mobility, and Princess Cruise Lines.

Colin is a clinical hypnotherapist and hypnosis instructor certified by the American Council of Hypnotist Examiners and also holds a bachelors degree in genetics and chemistry.

Colin has been a guest expert on radio and television, and he's been featured in *Psychology Today* as well as other magazines both in print and on-line.

Today Colin helps companies manage change to improve performance, using Success through Manipulation training. He also teaches people how to become stage hypnotists and travels the world performing fun, entertaining stage hypnosis shows.